Table Saw
Fundamentals

Rick Peters

Hearst Books
A Division of Sterling Publishing Co., Inc.
New York

Produced by How-2 Media Inc.

Design: Triad Design Group

Cover Design: Celia Fuller

Photography: Christopher J. Vendetta

Contributing Writer: Cheryl A. Romano

Illustrations: Triad Design Group

Copy Editor: Barbara McIntosh Webb

Page Layout: Triad Design Group

Index: Nan Badgett

Library of Congress Cataloging-in-Publication Data
Peters, Rick.
    Popular mechanics workshop. Table saw fundamentals : the complete guide / Rick Peters.
        p. cm.
    Includes index.
    ISBN 1-58816-367-9
    1. Woodwork. 2. Circular Saws. I. Title.
    TT180.P46 2004
    684'.083--dc22
                                                    2004052645

10 9 8 7 6 5 4 3 2 1

Published by Hearst Books
A Division of Sterling Publishing Co., Inc.
387 Park Avenue South, New York, NY 10016

Popular Mechanics is a trademark owned by Hearst Magazines Property, Inc., in USA, and Hearst Communications, Inc., in Canada. Hearst Books is a trademark owned by Hearst Communications, Inc.

www.popularmechanics.com

Distributed in Canada by Sterling Publishing
c/o Canadian Manda Group, 165 Dufferin Street
Toronto, Ontario, Canada M6K 3HG

Distributed in Australia by Capricorn Link (Australia) Pty. Ltd.
P.O. Box 704, Windsor, NSW 2756 Australia

Manufactured in China

ISBN 1-58816-367-9

Contents

ACKNOWLEDGMENTS

For all their help, advice, and support, I offer thanks to:

Christopher Vendetta, ace photographer, for taking great photos in less-than-desirable conditions (my dusty workshop).

Jim Brewer and Lisa Agostoni of Freud Tools for supplying photos, technical data, and their high-quality saw blades and dado sets.

Laura Geoghegan, with WMH Tool Group (Jet Equipment and Tools), for supplying photos, technical information, and their well-crafted contractor's saw.

Jason Feldner at Bosch Power Tools for providing technical information, photos, and their superbly designed bench-top table saw.

Chad Corley with Porter-Cable for supplying photos, technical information, and their bench-top table saw.

Leigh Bailey with Hitachi for supplying images, technical information, and their easy-to-use bench-top table saw.

The folks at DeWalt Tools for providing images, technical information, and their well-thought-out bench-top table saw.

David Watkins of Triton Manufacturing & Design Company for supplying their super-versatile multi-stand.

Karen Slatter at Benchdog for supplying technical information and images as well as their sturdy and easy-to-use Bench-Loc and featherboard.

Jerry Jaksha of Grip-Tite/Mesa Vista Design for sending us technical information, photos, and one of their hard-working Grip-Tite featherboards.

Doug Hicks with August Home Publishing for providing the photo of the Woodsmith aluminum box-joint jig.

The following companies also provided photos for use in this book:

Incra/Taylor Design Group, Inc.
SawStop, LLC
Delta Woodworking Machinery
Biesemeyer Woodworking Tools

Special thanks also to:

Rob Lembo and the staff at Triad Design Group, for their superb illustrations and page layout talents that are evident in every page of this book.

Barb Webb, copyediting whiz, for ferreting out mistakes and gently suggesting corrections.

Heartfelt thanks to my constant inspiration: Cheryl, Lynne, Will, and Beth, for putting up with the craziness that goes with writing a book and living with a woodworker: late nights, wood everywhere, noise from the shop, and sawdust footprints in the house.

INTRODUCTION

The single tool that transports the average wood tinkerer into a woodworker is the table saw. Whether it's a small bench-top saw or a heavy cast-iron cabinet saw, this one tool opens up a world of woodworking possibilities. No longer will you have to ask someone at a home center to cut a sheet of plywood, only to find out that the cut is off. Projects don't have to be designed around the precut sizes of dimension lumber—you can cut lumber to any width or length you want. And you won't have to wrestle with clamps, a sawhorse, and a circular saw to make the cut. All of a sudden your cutting accuracy and joint-making ability will be escalated to a higher level. And all this from just a single tool.

In these pages, you'll discover all that a table saw can do: how it can cut boards to length and width with super precision, how to use it to cut simple joints like grooves, dadoes, rabbets, and miters. We'll cover where to locate your saw in the shop, how to prepare for making a cut, and even how to work with non-wood materials. Then we'll show you how to tackle some of the more challenging jobs a table saw can handle, such as cutting compound miters and coves, making stopped cuts, and resawing. Then we'll delve into joinery, everything from locking rabbets and lap joints to cutting tenons and raised panels. Advanced techniques like making molding, kerf-bending, and even jointing on the table saw are covered in detail.

We'll start by taking you through the various types of table saws available and show you what to look for—and what to look out for—whether you're buying your first or upgrading to another. Then we'll take you through the myriad accessories available to make your table saw even more versatile. This is followed by a chapter of easy-to- make jigs for your table saw. Then, to keep your new or old table saw running in tip-top condition, there's an entire chapter devoted to maintenance: from cleaning and sharpening blades to step-by-step instructions on how to adjust the often-misunderstood trunion.

Finally, the last chapter offers projects you can build that showcase a variety of techniques described in the book. We're sure you'll want to hurry off to the shop after you've paged through this book.

Make sure to follow all tool manufacturers' safety guidelines—and enjoy your woodworking.

—James Meigs
Editor-in-Chief, Popular Mechanics

1 Choosing a Table Saw

The table saw is the heart of most woodworking shops — and for good reason. By itself a table saw is capable of an amazing variety of tasks. This hard-working tool is used for ripping, crosscutting, miters, bevels, joinery — even shaping edges. When you start adding any of the huge array of accessories available for a table saw, this tool can do a whole lot more: everything from cutting box joints and tapering legs to making raised panels and bending wood.

For many woodworkers, the purchase of a table saw is a once-in-a-lifetime event. A quality table saw can run anywhere from $750 to well over $1,000. With this kind of investment, it only makes sense to learn as much as you can about the different types and models of saws available so that you can compare features and make an intelligent purchase. This chapter delves into the myriad options out there so you can do just that.

Table saws have come a long way from the original saws that were basically a blade mounted under a tabletop. Today's saws offer a dizzying variety of options such as built-in outfeed support, super-precise rip fences, and even ports for dust collection to help whisk harmful dust away from your lungs.

Types of Table Saws

There are three main types of table saws to choose from: bench-top saws, contractor's saws, and cabinet saws, see photo below right. Bench-top, contractor's, and cabinet saws all basically have the same parts — what's different is the size and quality. At its simplest, a table saw consists of a blade attached to the shaft of a motor. The blade protrudes through a slot in the table and is raised or lowered as needed. It can also be tilted from side to side for bevel cuts. Most woodworkers prefer a saw where the blade tilts to the left since this angles the blade away from both the rip fence and their hands, see the drawing below.

For rip cuts, a fence attaches to the table so it's parallel to the blade. This fence rides on round or square bars, or extrusions that attach to the front and back top edge of the table. For crosscuts, slots in the table accept a miter gauge (and other accessories such as a tenoning jig). Bench-top and contractor's saws attach to a steel base to bring the table up to a comfortable working height. Cabinet saws usually have a closed-in base, housing a motor that connects to the saw arbor with V-belts. Closing in the base like this reduces noise and also allows for efficient dust collection. On contractor's saws, the motor is usually mounted on the back of the table saw and again is connected to the saw arbor with a belt. Bench-top saws typically have the blade attached directly to the motor shaft.

Blade diameter and arbor size

Table saws are generally classified by the diameter of the blade they can accept, see the bottom left photo. This in turn will determine the saw's maximum cut. Most contractor's and cabinet saws take a 10" blade and can cut stock over 3" thick. In the past, bench-top saws often took only an 8" blade (or smaller) and could handle only stock up to 2" thick. Today, most bench-top saws accept a 10" blade and so are theoretically capable of making cuts similar to those on a contractor's or cabinet saw. But because their motors are so much smaller, this isn't the case (see page 12 for more on motors). Note: Most new saws come with a $5/8$" arbor to accept the standard arbor hole in blades — $5/8$". Older saws may have larger or smaller arbors; some new large cabinet saws have 1" arbors, but these are primarily used in production shops.

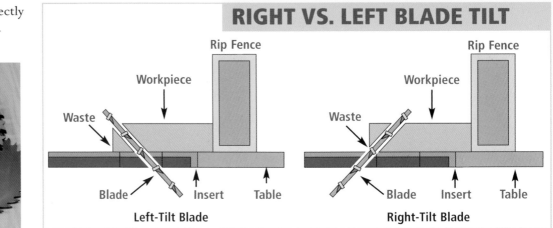

RIGHT VS. LEFT BLADE TILT

Rip Fence — Workpiece — Waste — Blade — Insert — Table

Left-Tilt Blade

Rip Fence — Workpiece — Waste — Blade — Insert — Table

Right-Tilt Blade

Bench-Top Saws

A bench-top saw like the one shown in the top photo is a good choice for a woodworker with limited space. These saws typically have smaller motors and are direct-drive; that is, the blade connects directly to the motor shaft. Because of this, they're good for light to medium jobs and should not be used for heavy work such as ripping thick stock. If you must do heavy work with this type of saw, slow down your feed rate to keep the small motor from bogging down. Woodworkers who work primarily on small to medium-sized projects (like birdhouses, or model making) find these smaller saws quite sufficient. Most portable power tool manufacturers now offer a bench-top saw, and many come with a collapsible stand. This has made bench-top saws more popular with carpenters and trim carpenters, since the tools fit better in a truck and are lighter and easier to carry around.

BENCH-TOP SAW ANATOMY

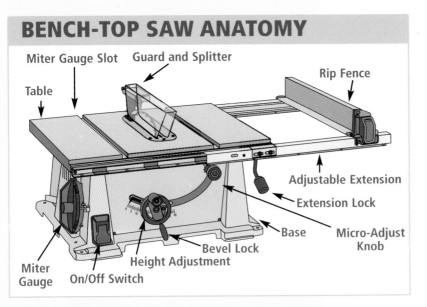

Miter Gauge Slot
Guard and Splitter
Table
Rip Fence
Adjustable Extension
Extension Lock
Base
Micro-Adjust Knob
Bevel Lock
Height Adjustment
Miter Gauge
On/Off Switch

BENCH-TOP SAW OPTIONS

Built-in storage. Because the cases of many bench-top saws are plastic, savvy manufacturers have molded in features like the blade storage shown here. Larger saw manufacturers could take a lesson from these smaller saws.

Side support. Because their table surfaces are generally smaller than that of their larger cousins, most bench-top saws provide alternative ways to support your workpiece. The pull-out side support shown here is common on most saws.

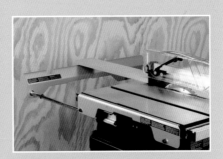

Outfeed support. Support behind the saw table is essential to support a workpiece after it has been cut. Virtually all the bench-top saws now being made provide outfeed support (like the one shown here), or it's available as an add-on.

Contractor's Saws

The next step up from a bench-top saw is the "contractor's" saw, like the one shown in the top photo. These saws are rugged, portable, and hardworking and have become extremely popular with contractors (hence the name). A contractor's saw is identifiable by its rear-mounted motor. Mounting the motor like this makes it easy for a framer or trim carpenter to set the saw (sans legs) on a pair of sawhorses and go right to work. This durable and modestly priced saw is the most popular choice for many woodworkers. Saw manufacturers now offer contractor's saws with large tables and super-accurate fences. A well-tuned contractor's saw can rival the performance of a cabinet saw (see page 11) — and they cost hundreds less.

The saw case on a contractor's saw is made of sheet metal, rather than the plastic cases on most bench-top saws. The saw table is heavy cast iron, and the extension wings on both sides of the table may be either cast iron or stamped metal. The guide rails that accept the rip fence are typically steel tubes. Precision rip fences replace these tubes with extruded rails that let the rip fence lock on in a more positive fashion, thereby increasing accuracy.

ANATOMY OF A CONTRACTOR'S SAW

Miter Gauge

Blade Guard and Splitter

Miter Gauge Slot

Rip Fence

Table Extension

Rear Guide Bar

Front Guide Bar

On/Off Switch

Height-Adjustment Wheel and Lock

Fence Lock

Bevel Adjusment Wheel and Lock

Bevel Scale

Open Metal Stand

Cabinet Saws

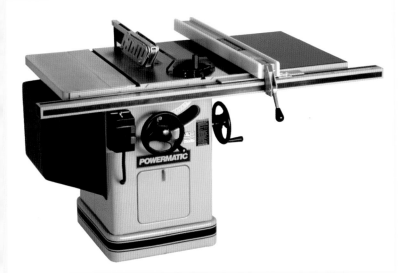

For many woodworkers, the ultimate table saw for their shop is the cabinet saw (often called a tilting-arbor saw or a stationary saw), like the one shown in the top photo. Cabinet saws feature a closed-in base, a large motor (ranging anywhere from 3-hp to over 7-hp), and heavy-duty castings. These saws cost in the $1,200 to $1,500 range and are hard to justify for the occasional woodworker. If you do a lot of woodworking (or can just plain afford it), consider buying a cabinet saw. A quality cabinet saw is vibration-free and cuts through even the thickest stock with ease. You'll notice a big difference in performance if you've used only a contractor's or bench-top saw in the past. A cabinet saw is generally more accurate that the other saw types and will last a lifetime if maintained properly.

ANATOMY OF A TILTING-ARBOR SAW

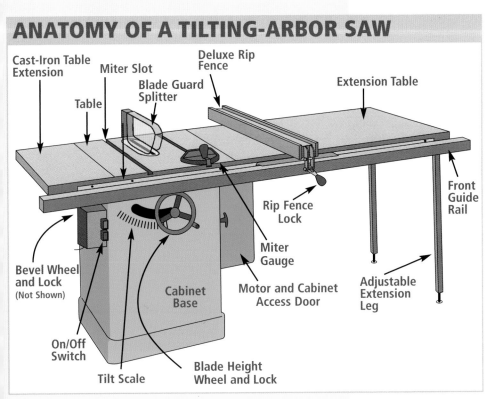

Cast-Iron Table Extension

Miter Slot

Deluxe Rip Fence

Table

Blade Guard Splitter

Extension Table

Front Guide Rail

Rip Fence Lock

Miter Gauge

Bevel Wheel and Lock (Not Shown)

Cabinet Base

Motor and Cabinet Access Door

Adjustable Extension Leg

On/Off Switch

Tilt Scale

Blade Height Wheel and Lock

Another huge advantage a cabinet saw offers over a contractor's saw or a bench-top saw has to do with the enclosed base. Sure it looks better, but the big deal about an enclosed base is that it makes dust collection a snap. Most cabinet saws have a built-in port so that all you have to do is hook up a vacuum, a portable dust collector, or a whole-shop collector, and the dust will be whisked away. This is especially important now that OSHA (Occupational Safety & Health Administration) has classified wood dust as a carcinogen.

Table Saw Motors

Next to blade diameter, the second most common way to classify a table saw is by its motor size, defined by its horsepower rating. The size of the motor will have a huge impact on a saw's ability to make a cut — especially in dense hardwoods, wet lumber, and thick stock. In cases like these, a small motor will bog down and often stall. Motors used for table saws are classified as one of two types: universal or induction. A universal motor has brushes and commutators and is widely used in portable power tools like routers and circular saws. Induction motors are used in contractor's and cabinet saws; they don't have brushes, and run off of AC power.

woodworkers (right photo). If, though, you tend to work with thick stock and/or work a saw hard, you're better off getting a saw with a larger motor. A typical cabinet saw uses a 3-hp induction motor that can plow through almost anything in a single pass. An item to note: 3-hp saws typically require 220 volts to operate. If your shop has only 110 volts, stick with a contractor's saw — they require only 110 volts (but it's a good idea to have the saw on its own 20-amp breaker).

Universal motors

Universal motors are compact and have a high starting torque (left photo). They run at high rpm and handle varying loads well; they're used in bench-top table saws. The downside to these motors is that they don't offer nearly the continuous load capabilities of an induction motor. This means they stall easily when making an aggressive cut, cutting into thick stock or dense woods. In most cases, you can still make the cut as long as you decrease the rate at which the wood is fed into the blade. Often, this slower feed rate is so slow that it'll cause burning. But when a universal motor is continuously bogged down like this, there's a very real danger of burning out the motor. Cuts like this are better left for a saw fitted with an induction motor.

Induction motors

Induction motors are heavy and bulky, but powerful — and virtually maintenance-free. Most have winding taps that allow you to wire the motor for 110 or 220-volt operation. Most contractor's saws use a $1^1/_2$-hp induction motor — big enough for most

HORSEPOWER 101

Horsepower is the amount of work done over time. Generally, when used to describe a tool, horsepower is an indication of how capable the tool is of performing its tasks. The rated horsepower of a tool is usually the torque level at which the motor can be run continuously without getting so hot that the winding insulation breaks down.

No motor produces usable horsepower unless it is slowed down by applying a mechanical load. With a universal motor, the horsepower is often labeled as "developed" horsepower. This is an attempt to mislead the consumer into thinking that products are more capable than they really are. Developed horsepower may be 2 to 5 times the continuous duty rating of a motor. The term "develops 3 hp" is meaningless marketing hype — use the amperage rating instead; as a rule of thumb, the higher the amperage, the more powerful the motor. (Amperage ratings can be found on the motor label.)

Rip Fence and Miter Gauge

When it comes to cutting accuracy, the two most important items on a table saw are the rip fence and the miter gauge (assuming the saw is adjusted properly; see Chapter 6 for table saw alignment). The rip fence is used to guide cuts generally made with the grain, to cut a board to a narrower width. The miter gauge is used to cut a board across its grain, to create a shorter piece. Both the rip fence and the miter gauge are commonly used for cutting joinery ranging from simple grooves and dadoes to more complex tenons and box joints. When choosing a saw, pay particular attention to these two items.

Add-on rip fence

There are two common ways to lock a rip fence in place. The method used by an add-on fence (middle left photo) locks the fence head onto the front guide rail only. The rear guide rail serves only to support the other end of the fence. Because the fence head is large and hooks onto a special extruded rail, these systems are very accurate, once adjusted. An accurate add-on rip fence can make all the difference between an average project and an extraordinary one. Since the table saw is used along with the jointer and planer to produce square stock to begin with, it's imperative the rip fence be equal to the task. If you're off even half a degree, your joints won't fit, boards won't glue up properly, and your projects (and you) will suffer. For more on add-on fences, see page 31.

Standard rip fence

On most standard rip fences, the fence is clamped either to the front and rear guide rails or to the edges of the saw top when the fence lock is activated (top left photo). Typically, a rod runs through the fence and attaches to a clamp pad on the rear end of the fence. When the fence lock is toggled, the rod pulls the pad backwards to squeeze the saw top or guide rails and lock the fence in place. The problem with many of these systems is that it's easy for the fence to "rack" out of position, resulting in a tapered cut. See pages 146–147 for tips on aligning a rip fence. Note that on many bench-top saws, the manufacturers have added a support to the fence to guide a workpiece when the fence is extended out past the saw top, as shown in the inset photo above.

Miter gauge

The miter gauge on table saws is adequate for most work. As long as you fine-tune the stops (see page 148), it'll do for most close-tolerance work as well. Just make sure there's no slop in the miter gauge bar — that is, you can't wiggle it from side to side as shown in the bottom left photo. If there is play, see page 149. For the ultimate in accuracy there are a number of high-quality after-market miter gauges available, see page 31.

Fit and Finish

Although not usually linked directly to a saw's performance, the fit and finish of a saw can have a profound impact on how accurately the saw cuts and how enjoyable it is to use. Fit and finish is the phrase used to describe how well saw parts fit together, how well-machined the parts are, and how smoothly the parts work together.

Rough castings not only don't look good, but they can also lead to inaccuracy and accidents. If a saw top isn't smooth, any variations will telegraph into your projects. Additionally, a rough casting can catch on a workpiece or hand, resulting in a ruined workpiece or a serious cut.

The only way to learn about a saw's fit and finish is to experience it first-hand. If you're shopping for a table saw, go to your local home center and check out what they have to offer. Likewise, woodworking shows are an excellent way to get your hands on various saws. Things to pay particular attention to are the saw top, the extension wings, and the control castings.

Saw top

Often overlooked, the quality, type, and size of the table of a table saw is an important feature worth looking into (top photo). Since the saw tops on most contractor's and cabinet saws are cast iron, it's also important that the top be true and flat. You can check this by placing a long metal rule or level on edge diagonally on the saw top. Look for any gaps between the rule and top, and then switch to the opposite diagonal and check. Variations will have to be removed by having the top machined flat at a machine shop. As this can be expensive, make sure to check this and return any saw with gaps.

Further ways to protect a saw's surface are to machine grooves in the top (like the Hitachi saw shown in the bottom photo) or to apply a protective rubber coating to the top (like the DeWalt saw in the bottom photo). Note: The slots in the saw top are also important. T-shaped slots capture the miter gauge over much of its travel, preventing it from tipping up and causing a nasty accident.

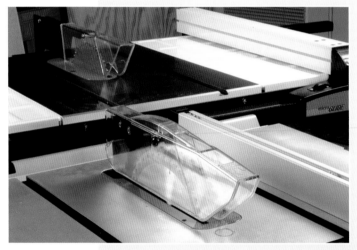

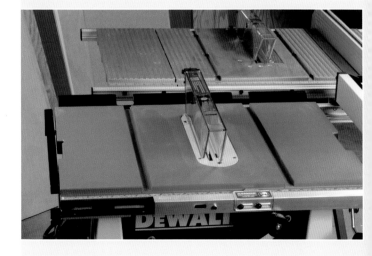

The saw tops on most bench-top saws are aluminum for two reasons: It's light, and it won't rust like cast iron. Both are important for saws that are often left outdoors at worksites or in the back of a truck.

Extension wings

To further extend the working surface of the top, most saw types have extension wings attached to each side. These may be stamped metal (at top in the top left photo), or cast iron (bottom of top left photo). If you're looking for extra rigidity, with the added benefit of dampened vibrations, consider paying the extra for cast-iron wings. Note: The top on most bench-top saws is a single unit; no wings are used, although side and outfeed supports can usually be purchased as accessories.

Control castings

Since you'll be constantly reaching for them, the control wheels (blade height and blade tilt) of a saw must be both sturdily made and comfortable to use. Metal wheels will hold up better over time, but must be machined well to be comfortable (middle photo). Plastic wheels (bottom photo) tend to be comfortable, but won't hold up as well as metal wheels. The control wheels on most contractor's and cabinet saws are cast or machined iron or steel. Bench-top saws usually have plastic controls to minimize the weight of the saw.

Safety Features

If you've ever flipped through a table saw manual, you've probably noticed that the first three to five pages are devoted to safety warnings. That's because regardless of the safety features built into a saw, it's a dangerous tool. Most cutting operations will bring one or both of your hands close to a spinning blade that's more than capable of severing fingers. This is why it's so important to take a close look at the safety features of any saw you're considering purchasing.

Warning: All the safety features in the world will not protect you if you don't protect yourself (see pages 32–33), keep the safety devices tuned and in full operating order, and use your head when cutting. With time, most woodworkers develop an "inner voice" that they hear when a cut seems unsafe. Woodworkers with all their fingers stop and listen to this voice and find a safer way to make the cut. Woodworkers who don't listen often end up with nicknames like "Stumpy."

The three primary safety features to look for on a table saw are the blade guard, the splitter/pawl assembly, and dust collection. Although dust collection may not seem like a safety feature, a good collection system will not only keep sawdust from interfering with your cuts, possibly causing an accident, but it will also keep dust out of your eyes and lungs.

Blade guards

Blade guards are made of high-impact plastic and are there to keep your fingers away from the blade. The front ends are angled so that when a workpiece is pushed into the guard, it'll automatically lift up and ride on the workpiece.

Look for two things here. First, make sure the guard can be pivoted completely out of your way (like the one shown below left) to make changing blades and setting up cuts easier. Guards that don't pivot out of the way, like the one shown in the bottom right photo, often end up being removed and left off. Second, look for a guard that's easy to remove for tasks like making cuts that don't pass all the way through the workpiece (such as a dado or groove). Here again, if it's a real pain to remove and install the guard, odds are it won't get reinstalled once it has been removed: This is just asking for an accident.

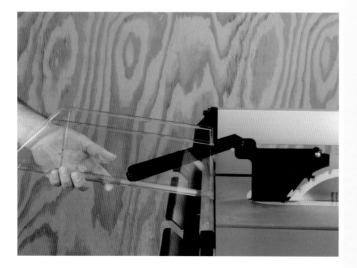

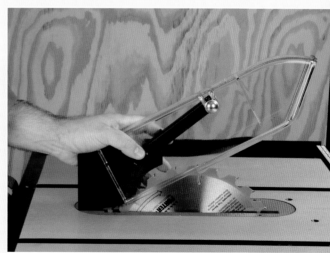

Splitter/pawl assemblies

The blade guards on most saws attach to the splitter/pawl assembly via a hinged support bar. And the splitter/pawl assembly attaches to the saw at the rear of the saw, down through the throat plate, or both ways. The splitter portion of the assembly is designed to keep the waste part of the workpiece from binding against the ripped portion after the blade cuts the kerf. To work properly, the splitter must be positioned directly behind the blade, see page 44. The pawls, commonly referred to as anti-kickback pawls, are barbed, spring-tensioned levers that allow wood to pass in one direction only. If the workpiece binds, or tries to kick backwards, the barbs of the pawls dig into the surface of the work-piece to prevent this. You'll find different kinds of pawls out there: some with many, small barbs (top photo) and some with fewer, larger barbs (middle photo). We've found that pawls with multiple smaller barbs tend to catch the work faster, but the larger barbs hold the workpiece better. In either case, the barbs must be kept sharp to work, see page 45.

Dust collection

The final safety feature worth looking at is dust collection. The type of saw determines how well dust can be whisked away. Bench-top saws usually have plastic shrouds that cover the blade, and funnel dust to a port that can be hooked up to a shop vacuum or a dust bag (far left bottom photo). These work quite well on most saws. Contractor's saws pose a real challenge for dust control. Although most manufacturers do offer a dust port, it attaches under the blade and will remove only dust that falls through (middle bottom photo). Suction is poor here, as the back of the case is wide open because of the rear-mounted motor. Since the cabinet of a cabinet saw is totally enclosed, these saws generally offer the best solution for dust collection (far right bottom photo).

Ergonomics

The final feature to look at when considering a table saw is ergonomics. Webster's defines ergonomics as "an applied science concerned with the characteristics of people that need to be considered in designing and arranging things that they use in order that people and things will interact most effectively and safely." When related to power tools, this basically means how easy and comfortable a tool is to use. Because there are a number of moving parts that need to be adjusted often on a table saw, it's important to check these out on a saw you're interested in. Just like checking out a saw's fit and finish, the only way to get a feel for its ergonomics is to get your hands on the saw — literally. Visit a home center, check out your friend's saw, or take a day trip to a woodworking show — it'll be time well spent. Operate the rip fence and miter gauge (see page 13), the blade guard and splitter/pawl assembly (see pages 16–17), the power switch (see below), and the blade-tilt and blade-height controls (see page 19).

Power switch

The location of the power switch and how it toggles on and off will be something you notice every time you use a saw. The switch should be located up front for easy access, preferably mounted directly under the guide rail (right photo below). The switch should be easy to turn on, but more importantly very easy to turn off in case of an emergency. Paddle-style switches like the one in the bottom left photo can be slapped off with a knee. If you have kids, look for a power switch that offers a removable key or can be locked in the off position.

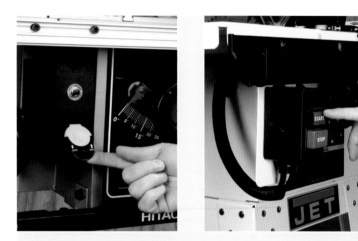

EMERGENCY STOPS

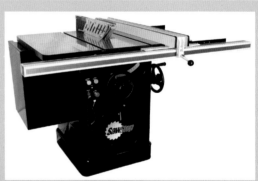

Imagine you're cutting a board when suddenly your hand slips and runs into the blade. The result is a serious injury, often an amputation of one or more fingers. Accidents like that happen to over 90,000 people a year in the United States. A new saw (shown in the photo at right) developed by SawStop (www.sawstop.com) can minimize the severity of these injuries.

SawStop saws include an electronic safety system that detects when a person accidentally contacts a moving blade (left photo). A fast-acting brake then stops the blade so quickly that the person typically gets only a small nick instead of a serious injury. SawStop demonstrates their system by pushing a hot dog into a spinning blade, as if the hot dog were a misplaced finger. The system immediately detects when the hot dog touches the blade, and then stops the blade in about 3 to 5 milliseconds, leaving the hot dog with only a scratch.

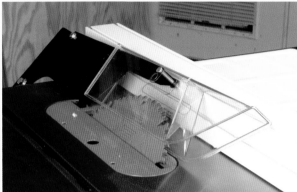

Blade-tilt control

Not only is it important to get a feel for the hand wheel for blade tilt, but it's also important to tilt the saw blade through its full motion so that you feel how smoothly the mechanism works and also which way the blade tilts. As we mentioned previously, a

blade that tilts away from the rip fence and the operator's hands (photo at left) is preferred by most woodworkers over a blade that tilts toward the fence and the operator's hands (top left photo).

Blade-height control

Even more so than the blade tilt, the blade-height mechanism is something you'll be reaching for on almost every cut. It's important that the blade-height mechanism be smooth and easy to lock in place; we noticed that some of the bench-top saws do not have a lock for blade height. Also, the location and type of control is critical. A good blade-height control will be fully accessible and easy to turn (photo at left). A blade-height control that's inferior is located so that your hand or wrist will strike the guide rail or saw top as you turn it, like the one shown in the photo below. This will get way beyond annoying

after you've used the saw for just a short period of time.

■ RECOMMENDATIONS

As with any tool, choosing a table saw is a very personal thing. Yes, it's a good idea to pore over the various specifications of different saws like motor size, blade diameter, arbor size, and cutting capacities; but there's no substitute for getting your hands on the models that interest you. Like most woodworkers, the type of saw you'll purchase will depend primarily on what you can spend and how much space you have. Additionally, the type of work you do — or plan to do — will have an impact on which saw you buy.

If you plan on only tinkering around in the shop every now and then and making small to medium projects like clocks, jewelry boxes, or children's toys, a bench-top saw will serve you well. But if there are larger projects on the horizon such as chests, chairs, or bookcases, consider stepping up to a contractor's saw. You'll find that this style of saw will handle most woodworking tasks.

If money and space are not issues, by all means purchase a cabinet saw. Your only tough decision here will be whether to get a tilt-left or a tilt-right. Most woodworkers prefer a tilt-left saw, since the blade tilts away from the rip fence for bevel cuts.

If you're on a budget (like most of us), a contractor's saw is a good choice. We would, however, recommend that you invest in a quality after-market rip fence, as this can make a huge difference in accuracy. Finally, if space and/or money matter, consider a smaller bench-top version (or if you need more power, buy a contractor's saw and spring for a mobile base).

Bench-top table saws. All of the bench-top saws listed in the chart, opposite, use a universal motor ranging from 13 to 15 amps. Their rpm varies from 3,650 up to 5,000. All but one of the saws utilize a 10" blade; they all have $5/8$" arbors. Maximum cutting and ripping capacity varies widely, so pay special attention to these specifications when comparing different models. If space is a concern, look for a model that offers a collapsible stand and/or a mobile base.

Contractor's table saws. The chart on the opposite page lists six of the most popular contractor's saws. All but one come with a $1^1/2$-horsepower induction motor, and they all accept 10"-diameter blades with a $5/8$" arbor hole. The maximum cutting capacities are very similar, but ripping capacity varies tremendously based on the type of rip fence system you buy.

Cabinet table saws. Cabinet table saws offer the most options for motors. Sizes vary from 3 to $7^1/2$ horsepower and typically require 220 volts. Most are available in both single and three-phase. Typical blade diameter is 10", but the larger saws can handle larger blades; arbor size is still usually $5/8$". Maximum cut and rip capacity vary from saw to saw, see the chart opposite.

BENCH-TOP TABLE SAWS

Brand	Model	Motor amps	Motor rpm	Blade diameter	Arbor size	Max. cut 90 degrees	Max. cut 45 degrees	Ripping capacity
Craftsman	21825	15.0	–	10"	5/8"	3"	2 1/2"	24"
Delta	TS200	13.0	4,700	10"	5/8"	3"	2 1/2"	9 1/2"
DeWalt	DW744	13.0	3,650	10"	5/8"	3 1/8"	2 1/4"	24 1/2"
Hitachi	C10RA2	15.0	5,000	10"	5/8"	3"	2 1/2"	15 3/4"
Makita	2702	15.0	4,600	8 1/4"	5/8"	2 11/16"	1 3/4"	22"
	2703	15.0	4,600	10"	5/8"	3 9/16"	2 1/2"	22"
Porter-Cable	3812	15.0	5,000	10"	5/8"	3 1/4"	–	24 1/2"
Ryobi	BTS10	13.0	4,800	10"	5/8"	3"	2"	9 1/2"
	BTS20	15.0	4,800	10"	5/8"	3 5/8"	2 1/2"	27"
Skil	3400	15.0	5,000	10"	5/8"	3"	2 1/2"	12 1/4"

CONTRACTOR'S TABLE SAWS

Brand	Model	Motor hp	Motor rpm	Blade diameter	Arbor size	Max. cut 90 degrees	Max. cut 45 degrees	Ripping capacity
Craftsman	22859	1 1/2	–	10"	5/8"	3 3/8"	2 1/4"	30"
	22839	1 1/2	–	10"	5/8"	3 3/8"	2 1/8"	24"
Delta	36-444	1 1/2–2	3,000	10"	5/8"	3 1/8"	2 1/8"	30"–50"
DeWalt	DW746	1 3/4	3,000	10"	5/8"	3 1/8"	2 1/8"	30"–52"
Jet	JWTS-10JF	1 1/2	4,000	10"	5/8"	3 1/8"	2 1/8"	30"–50"
Powermatic	64A	1 1/2	4,500	10"	5/8"	3 1/4"	2 1/8"	30"–50"

CABINET TABLE SAWS

Brand	Model	Motor hp	Motor rpm	Blade diameter	Arbor size	Max. cut 90 degrees	Max. cut 45 degrees	Ripping capacity
Craftsman	22694	3	3,450	10"	5/8"	3"	2 1/8"	50"
Delta	36-830A	3	3,450	10"	5/8"	3 1/8"	2 1/8"	30"–50"
	36-51	5	3,450	10"	5/8"	3 1/8"	2 1/8"	30"–50"
	RT-40	7 1/2	3,000/4,500	14"/16"	1"	5 1/2"	4 1/8"	52"
Jet	JTAS-10	3–5	4,200	10"	5/8"	3 1/8"	2 1/8"	30"–50"
Jet	JTAS-12	3–5	4,200	12"	1"	4"	2 7/8"	30"–50"
Powermatic	66	3–5	3,600	10"	5/8"	3 1/8"	2 1/8"	30"–50"
	72A	3–5	3,600	14"	1"	5 1/8"	3 1/2"	30"–50"

2 Table Saw Accessories

How versatile is a particular tool? One of the better ways to determine this is to identify how many accessories are made for it. The more accessories there are, the more the tool can do. By this standard, in portable power tools the router is the king. There are more accessories built for the router than for almost all the other portable power tools combined. In the land of stationary tools, the table saw is the clear winner. And we're not talking about just blades here. Yes, there are hundreds of different types, styles, and sizes of saw blades available. But there's also a plethora of add-ons, jigs, and safety accessories available.

We'll look at the most common table saw accessories and help you decide what you need — and what you don't. We'll cover everything from saw blades and dado sets to molding heads, roller stands, and specialty jigs such as tenoning and box-joint jigs. Don't buy anything until you read this chapter.

There's an enormous array of accessories available for your table saw — some essential, some not. Accessories for the table saw include much more than just blades: Push sticks and other safety gear should head your list. Then you can pick up fun accessories like molding heads and dado sets that let you cut fancy moldings and intricate joinery.

Blade Basics

The number one accessory for a table saw is the saw blade. Blades are available in diameters ranging from 8" up to 16", with 10" being the most common. The hole in the center of the saw that fits over the saw arbor is usually ⁵/₈" in diameter, although other sizes are used. In particular, large-diameter arbors are used in large production cabinet saws, with motor sizes often above 5 hp. To select blades for your saw, you'll need to know about the different types, basic anatomy, tooth configurations, what specialty blades are available, and what they're for.

Blade materials

There are two types of materials used to make table saw blades: high-speed steel (HSS) and carbide (top photo). Although blades made solely of high-speed steel are inexpensive, they dull quickly and need to be resharpened frequently. The money you'd save on sharpening costs is better invested in a quality blade with carbide tips. That's because a carbide-tipped blade will stay sharper a whole lot longer than HSS — and they can be resharpened as well (just make sure you use a sharpening service that's experienced with carbide). The quality of the blade will have much to do with the thickness and quality of the carbide, so go with a name you can trust.

Saw blade anatomy

At its most basic, a saw blade is a disc of metal with a hole in the middle and teeth cut around its perimeter. In terms of a high-speed steel blade, this is still basically all there is. The teeth can be cut in a variety of tooth configurations (see page 25) and are set in alternate directions. High-speed steel teeth are "set" or bent alter-

nately away from the body of the blade. This produces a kerf that is wider than the body of the blade so that the blade can pass through the wood without binding. So in addition to being sharpened, an HSS blade will always need to be set in order to run true and not produce a bad cut. If just a single tooth is not set correctly — say, for instance, it is bent out too far from the blade body — this tooth will end up doing all the work, will dull extremely fast, and will end up tearing wood instead of slicing through it.

A carbide-tipped blade, on the other hand, does not need to be set: The carbide teeth brazed onto the blade body are wider than the body and will produce a kerf sufficient for the body to pass through. Advances in saw blade technology by cutting-edge manufacturers have improved performance of carbide-tipped blades tremendously. Two common advances are expansion slots and anti-vibration slots cut into the body of the blade, see the drawing below. Expansion slots reduce noise and let the blade expand and contract as needed as it heats in use. Anti-vibration slots reduce vibration and chatter to the point that stabilizers (see page 27) are not needed.

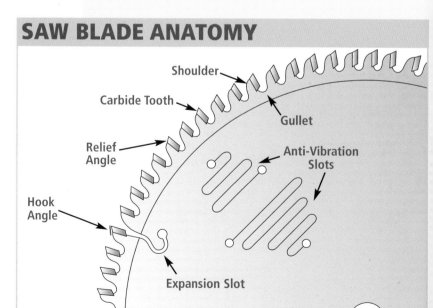

SAW BLADE ANATOMY

Shoulder

Carbide Tooth

Gullet

Relief Angle

Anti-Vibration Slots

Hook Angle

Expansion Slot

Arbor Hole

Tooth Configuration

The teeth on most carbide-tipped blades are set up into one of four common configurations: flat top grind, triple chip and flat grind, ATB (alternate tooth bevel), and ATB with raker, as shown in the top photo and drawing below.

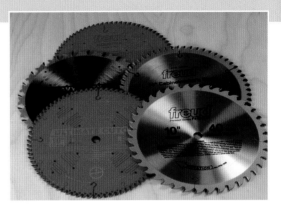

Flat top grind

Blades with flat top grind teeth are primarily used for ripping. That's because a flat tooth will cut much like a tiny plane blade. And this will produce a smooth cut only if you're cutting with the grain, as you do when ripping a piece of wood to size. If used for cross-grain cuts, this type of blade will produce a very jagged edge, especially on the face grain of the workpiece.

Triple chip with flat top

A triple chip blade has teeth that are similar to a flat top grind except that the corners of the teeth are knocked off to produce three cutting surfaces, or a triple chip tooth. The advantage with this configuration is that these teeth will tend to tear cross grain much less than a flat grind tooth. By slipping in a flat grind tooth every three or four teeth, you get a blade that rips smoothly and crosscuts fair.

Alternate tooth bevel

The teeth of an ATB blade are beveled in alternate directions every alternate tooth. This configuration closely approximates the blade of a crosscut saw. The sharply angled teeth act like small chisels to cleanly sever cross-grain fibers. This creates a smooth crosscut, but unfortunately doesn't do a very good job of ripping.

ATB with raker

Just like the triple chip with flat top, the ATB with raker is a compromise between ripping and crosscutting. By inserting a flat raker tooth every three or four beveled teeth, this blade does an adequate job of both ripping and crosscutting.

For general-purpose work, a combination blade is your best bet — we've found that a 40-tooth ATB with raker blade works well. But it's also a good idea to have both a true crosscut blade (ATB) and a ripping blade (flat top grind) on hand for the occasions when you need to rip or crosscut a lot of stock.

TOOTH CONFIGURATIONS

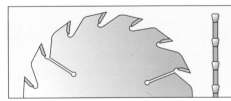

Flat Top Grind

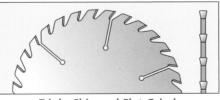

Triple Chip and Flat Grind

ATB and Raker

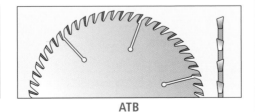

ATB

Blade Types

Rip blades

A rip blade provides smooth, fast rip cuts in both hardwoods and softwoods (top photo). The blade bodies tend to be thicker than other blades to create a rigid body that, when combined with sharp carbide teeth, will produce a cut edge that's ready to be glued — no jointing is needed. Rip blades generally have fewer teeth than other blades — anywhere from 16 to 24 on a 10" blade. The hook angle (see the drawing on page 24) is typically around 20 degrees. The hook angle is the angle at which the tooth is presented to the workpiece as if a line were drawn from the center of the arbor hole to the tip of the blade. Compare this with the hook angle of the crosscut blade below.

Crosscut blades

The teeth on a crosscut blade are usually alternate tooth bevel — and there are a lot of them (middle photo). Typical tooth count on a quality crosscut blade will vary from 60 to 80 teeth. The hook angle is usually around 2 degrees to create a slicing cut. The higher-tooth-count blades like the one shown here will produce a virtually chip-free cut that will be satin smooth.

Combination blades

Combination blades, often called general-purpose blades, are designed to make both rips and crosscuts (bottom photo). They do both well, but neither as well as the dedicated blades. The teeth on combination blades can be ATB, ATB with raker, or triple chip with flat top teeth. Tooth count is typically 40. Hook angle generally ranges from 13 degrees up to 18 degrees. Naturally, blade engineers are trying to find a midpoint between a 24-degree rip hook angle and the 3-degree crosscut hook angle. Since most woodworkers don't want to have to change blades when switching from a rip to a crosscut, this type of blade is the most common you'll find in most woodshop table saws.

PLYWOOD CUTTING BLADE

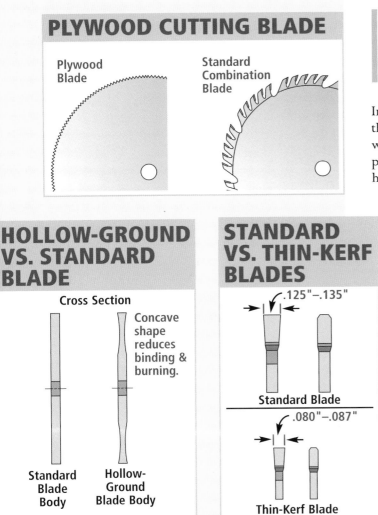

Plywood Blade

Standard Combination Blade

Specialty Blades

In addition to rip, crosscut, and combination blades, there are a number of specialty blades that you might want to consider adding to your blade arsenal — in particular, a plywood blade, a thin-kerf blade, and a hollow-ground blade.

HOLLOW-GROUND VS. STANDARD BLADE

Cross Section

Concave shape reduces binding & burning.

Standard Blade Body

Hollow-Ground Blade Body

STANDARD VS. THIN-KERF BLADES

.125"–.135"

Standard Blade

.080"–.087"

Thin-Kerf Blade

Plywood blade

Most plywood blades are high-speed steel because the teeth of the blade are small and very numerous, as shown in the top drawing. These tiny teeth do an excellent job of not tearing the fragile face veneers of plywood (see page 52 for more on plywood). Although there are carbide-tipped blades that are optimized for cutting plywood and other faced sheet stock such as melamine, they're quite expensive because the tooth count is typically 80.

Thin-kerf blade

Blades that cut leaving a thin kerf are gaining popularity with woodworkers as the cost of wood continues to rise. In addition to wasting less wood, a thin-kerf blade requires less power since it's cutting a thinner kerf, as shown in the near left drawing. The downside to these blades is that the bodies are thinner and not as rigid as standard blades. This means that they are prone to vibration, especially when used to cut thick or dense stock in a single pass.

Hollow-ground blade

For the most part, hollow-ground blades like the one shown in the middle left drawing have been replaced by thin-kerf blades. The idea behind a hollow-ground blade is simply that hollows are ground on each face of the blade body as shown. This reduces problems with binding and burning. Any thin-kerf or carbide-tipped blade will do the same thing.

BLADE STABILIZERS

Blade stabilizers, also called stiffening collars, are a set of precision machined and balanced plates that fit on both sides of a saw blade (photo at right). They not only improve the cut by reducing blade vibration, but they also help the saw to run quieter. They're particularly useful for the thinner-bodied thin-kerf blades. Reducing vibration also helps extend the life of the saw. Most stabilizers are designed for blades 7" in diameter and larger and are intended for use only with stationary saws.

Dado Sets

In addition to a good-quality combination blade, you'll want to get a dado set (top photo). Dado sets are basically two blades with chippers sandwiched in between. Varying the number of chippers changes the width of the dado. Fine adjustments can be made by adding or removing shims between the chippers, see below. Freud has just introduced a new dado set that lets you dial in the exact width you want — no shims required (top right photo). Of all the blades you'll use in your saw, a dado set has the greatest ability to chew up your hands. That's why we recommend buying a "safety" dado set. Freud makes a set that has kickback-reducing limiters on both the outer blades and the chippers that greatly reduce the danger of kickback from overfeeding.

Note that most dado blades are 8" or less in diameter. That's because when fitted with all cutters, they can remove a lot of wood. The manufacturers decrease the diameter so that you can't damage your saw by trying to take too hefty a cut (the smaller diameters are also safer).

Stacked set versus wobble blade

There are two basic types of dado cutters: a stacked set and a wobble blade, see the drawing at right. A stacked dado set consists of two outer blades and a set of chippers that are sandwiched in between the blades. Varying the number of chippers determines the width of the cut. For the best balance (and minimal vibration), it's important to install the chippers so they're spread out evenly along the perimeter of the blade. For

two chippers, install them perpendicular to each other; for three, space them out like those shown in the top drawing. A wobble blade sits in an adjustable collar at an angle. The width of the dado is adjusted by changing the angle of the blade. Although inexpensive, these blades produce curved bottoms unlike the more desired flat bottom that a dado set creates.

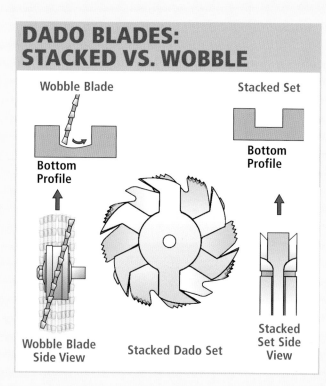

DADO BLADES: STACKED VS. WOBBLE

Wobble Blade

Stacked Set

Bottom Profile

Bottom Profile

Wobble Blade Side View

Stacked Dado Set

Stacked Set Side View

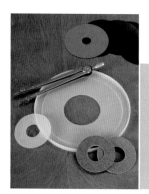

DADO SHIMS

You can fine-tune the width of a dado by inserting round shims between the chippers. These can be bought made from metal stock of varying thickness, or you can make your own: Try using the plastic lids from coffee cans or plastic laminate, as shown in the bottom left photo.

Molding Heads

If you don't have access to a router table or a shaper, you may want to consider purchasing a molding head like the one shown in the photo at left. Molding heads accept a wide variety of cutters (drawing below) and can virtually turn your table saw into a router or shaper capable of making intricate molding and even joints. Most molding sets come with a molding head that's slotted to accept a set of three matched cutters. Each cutter is fitted into a slot and then locked in place with a setscrew that passes through the hole in the cutter and threads into the body of the molding head.

Like a dado set, the knives of a molding head have the potential to cause severe damage if they come in contact with your hand. That's why it's important to use all safety devices, including push sticks to pass a workpiece over the revolving head (see page 88 for more on using a molding head). On the plus side, because the molding head is powered by a strong table saw motor, it can cut a joint or make a molding in a single pass. But as always, it's best to do this in multiple passes because this will put less strain on the saw motor and cutter knives and also produce a cleaner cut.

TYPICAL MOLDING CUTTER PROFILES

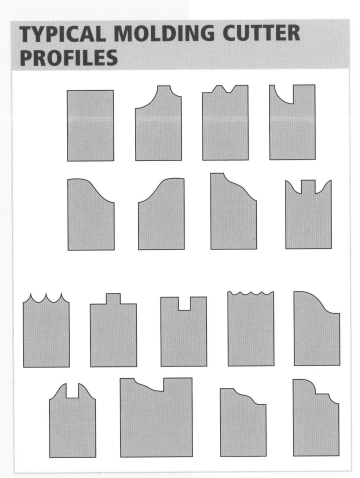

Table Extensions

There are a number of add-on table extensions you can purchase for your saw that can increase its capabilities and cutting capacity. The most common of these are an outfeed support and a router table insert.

Outfeed support

Cutting long stock or wide panels is a whole lot easier if the workpiece is supported during the cut. Support is especially vital after the cut on the outfeed side of table, since both the cut piece and the waste piece are in danger of tipping off the edge of table. Outfeed support is the solution to this potentially dangerous problem. Although you can use a roller stand (see page 35), a more stable option is an attached outfeed extension. There are a variety of these available. Most lift off (inset photo at right) or swing down out of the way (top photo at right) when they're not being used. This is especially handy in a shop tight on space.

Router table inserts

Another way to save space in a small shop is to combine tools. A nifty way to combine a router table with a table saw is to replace one of your table saw's extension wings with a router table insert, as shown in the middle photo. A number of enterprising router accessory manufacturers offer pre-made tables designed to fit a variety of saws. The table insert shown in the bottom photo is manufactured by Bench Dog (www.benchdog.com).

MOBILE BASES

Among the things you can do to improve a small shop or temporary shop (like one shared with a car) is to add a mobile base to your saw. You can make a mobile base yourself, or buy one. To make one, attach heavy-duty locking swivel rollers to a piece of plywood with cleats on the perimeter. Store-bought bases range from kits with brackets that accept 2-by lumber you cut to fit, all the way to customized bases for the saw and extension table like the one shown here. Even if you're not cramped for space, it's nice to be able to move your saw for cleaning and maintenance, or when you need to cut a particularly long or wide piece that isn't possible with your current saw location.

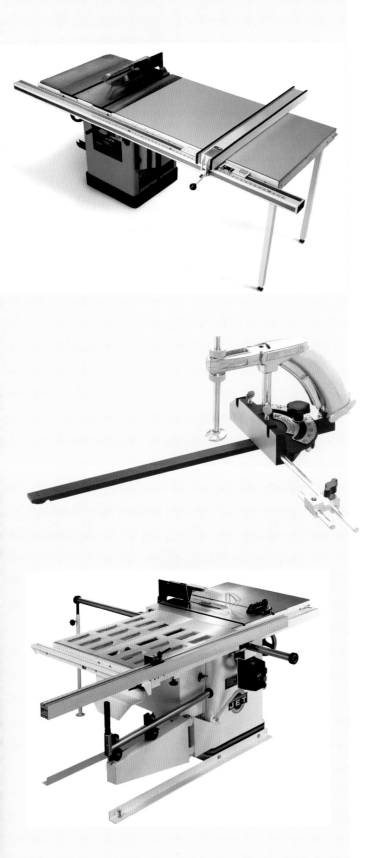

Precision Add-Ons

A finely tuned table saw with standard accessories can certainly produce quality cuts. But for the greatest precision, consider purchasing any of the precision add-ons shown here: a rip fence system, a clamping miter gauge, or a sliding table.

Rip fence systems

A precision rip fence system like the Biesmeyer fence shown in the top left photo is the number one add-on most woodworkers are willing to pay extra for. That's because the built-in measuring tape and easy-to-read indicator make it simple to slide and lock the fence at any measurement without having to reach for a tape measure (as long as the indicator is adjusted for the blade in the saw). In addition to having a super-positive locking system that keeps the fence solidly in place once adjusted, the extra-long fence helps support stock better after the cut.

Clamping miter gauge

The standard miter gauge that comes with most saws could use some improvement. Notably, a built-in clamp would be nice to keep a workpiece from shifting during a cut, and a stop system would be useful for making repeat cuts with extra precision. That's exactly what some tool accessory manufacturers have added to a standard gauge. Clamping miter gauges like the one shown in the middle photo are available through most mail-order woodworking companies, like Woodcraft Supply (www.woodcraft.com).

Sliding table

The ultimate precision add-on for a table saw is a sliding table like the Jet version shown in the bottom left photo. A properly adjusted sliding table is a joy to use. Not only is it capable of producing dead-on crosscuts, but it also can be used to rip and crosscut sheet stock to exact dimensions. If your shop space allows and you've got a thick wallet (these tables are quite expensive), consider adding this deluxe attachment to your saw.

Safety Add-Ons

The table saw is an amazingly versatile tool. But as we've mentioned throughout this book, it can be a dangerous tool if safety guards are not maintained and religiously used. Besides the standard safety gear that comes with your saw (most notably the saw guard and splitter/anti-kickback pawl assembly), there are additional safety add-ons you can buy to make your work at the table saw safe and enjoyable.

Premium blade guards

The blade guards on most table saws tend to get removed and then never replaced. Premium blade guards like the one shown in the top right photo are designed to combat this tendency. When not needed, the guard can simply be lifted up away from the

cut. For the next cut where the guard should be used, it's lowered into place. Some premium guard systems also have an integrated hose that hooks up your dust collector to capture dust as it comes off the saw blade.

Zero-clearance plates

An essential safety device when cutting narrow strips or small parts is a zero-clearance plate. You can buy one to fit a number of saws (photo at right), or make your own, see page 51. The idea is to eliminate the gap in the standard opening on both sides of the blade. Closing these gaps prevents parts from dropping between the throat plate and the blade, possibly causing an accident.

ANTI-KICKBACK ROLLERS AND POWER FEEDERS

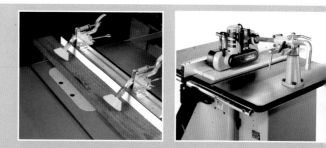

Two other safety devices that are particularly handy when ripping a lot of stock to width are a set of anti-kickback rollers (near right photo) or a power feeder (far right photo). Anti-kickback rollers attach to your rip fence and prevent a workpiece from kicking back. This is accomplished via spring-tensioned rollers that rotate in only one direction — the direction you'll be feeding the stock, see the drawing at right. If kickback does occur, the rubber wheels grip the stock and, since they can't rotate in reverse, they freeze the stock in place long enough for you to safely turn off your saw.

A power feeder is a separate motorized attachment that mounts to your saw top. A wide motor-driven belt grabs the workpiece and feeds it past the blade. Since no hands are needed once the belt grips the workpiece, this is the safest way you can make a cut. And since the belt travels in only one direction, kickback is prevented.

HOW ANTI-KICKBACK ROLLERS WORK

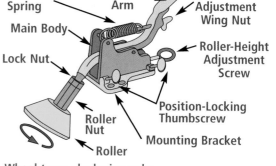

Roller Pressure Spring — Pivot Arm — Roller Pressure Adjustment Wing Nut

Main Body

Lock Nut — Roller-Height Adjustment Screw

Roller Nut — Position-Locking Thumbscrew

Roller — Mounting Bracket

Wheel turns clockwise only; it will not reverse to allow kickback.

Push sticks

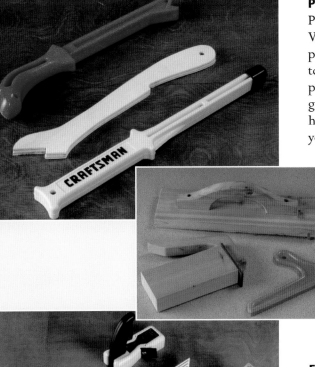

Push sticks are finger-savers — need we say more? Whether you make your own (see pages 98–99) or purchase them, push sticks (like those shown in the top photo) are designed to push a workpiece safely past a spinning blade. Of course for these to do any good, they have to be used. Keep a lot of these on hand, and use them whenever a cut would bring your hand close enough to contact the blade.

Push blocks

A variation of the push stick is the push block (middle photo). The difference between the two? A push block is wider and is useful when you need to both push the workpiece forward and apply downward pressure to keep the stock flat against the saw top. The top push block in the photo is identical to the one we use to feed stock when planing the face of a workpiece on the jointer.

Featherboards

Featherboards are used to apply pressure to a workpiece to keep it pressed firmly against a rip fence or saw top, see the photo at left. These are especially useful for operations that would normally bring your fingers too close to a blade: cutting a board on edge when cutting joinery, resawing (pages 68–69), or making raised panels (pages 90–91). You can buy a featherboard, or make your own (see pages 100–103).

BLADE-LOC

Fingers often get nicked when changing blades. One way to prevent this is to use a safety device just for changing blades like the Blade-Loc by Bench Dog (www.benchdog.com). Sure, you can use a scrap block to keep the blade from spinning when you loosen or tighten the arbor nut. But the advantage of Blade-Loc is that the saw teeth are completely covered by the device, so there's no chance of injury if the wrench slips and your hand makes contact with the blade. To use the Blade-Loc, simply lower it onto the blade and tighten or loosen the arbor nut. As soon as one of the plastic arms in the front and back of the Blade-Loc comes in contact with the saw top, it will prevent the saw blade from spinning.

Table Saw Jigs

You can do more with a table saw by using one of the many jigs made especially for it. Three of the more popular jigs are described below.

Tenoning jig

A tenoning jig like the one shown in the top photo is used to position a workpiece vertically for cutting tenons. These jigs range from simple non-adjustable versions that slide along or on the rip fence, to deluxe, fully adjustable multi-stop units like the one shown here. Not only will the tenoning jig shown here hold the workpiece in perfect position, but it also has two stops that, when set up, let you cut both cheeks of a tenon without removing the workpiece and repositioning it. For more on cutting tenons, see pages 79–82.

Incra miter jig

Another popular table saw jig is the Incra miter gauge jig shown in the middle photo. This miter jig has 364 positive angle stops in $1/2$-degree increments over a full plus- or minus-90-degree range. This system lets you miter with accuracy you didn't imagine was possible. An additional benefit: A set of built-in expansion slots lets you adjust both sides of the miter gauge bar to completely remove any side-to-side play.

Box-joint jig

If you're interested in building sturdy cases or boxes, consider picking up a box-joint jig like the one shown in the bottom photo. This extruded aluminum jig is available through mail-order woodworking catalogs or directly from the folks at Woodsmith who designed it (www.woodsmithstore.com). This jig features an adjustable key slot and replaceable backing strip that make it easy to cut accurate box joints. The micro-adjust feature of the jig allows you to "dial in" perfect-fitting box joints by adjusting the key position in increments of less than $1/64$". The unique replaceable plastic backing strip backs up your stock to eliminate chip-out.

Roller Stands

Inexpensive and extremely useful, a roller stand is an accessory no shop should be without. Roller stands are portable support for your table saw. They can be positioned behind the saw as outfeed support to catch a long workpiece, on the side for supporting long crosscuts or wide panels, or in front of the saw to help guide a long or wide workpiece safely into the saw. You can purchase a roller stand or build your own.

Manufactured roller stands

Several manufacturers make roller stands in a variety of shapes and sizes. The most common version is a single-roller stand like the one shown in the top photo. These stands usually collapse for storage, and one leg has a clamp that allows you to raise or lower the roller as needed. These stands are relatively inexpensive and work moderately well.

Shop-made stand

You can make your own roller stand using common lumber and some PVC pipe. See pages 104–109 for complete directions on how to make the roller stand shown in the middle photo. This stand features a set of four rollers that provide better support of a workpiece versus a single roller. As with any stand, the rollers can be raised or lowered as needed.

A ROLLER STAND WITHOUT ROLLERS?

A typical roller stand does a fair job of supporting a workpiece, but it does have a couple of inherent design flaws. First, if the roller isn't absolutely parallel to the back edge of the saw top, the roller will tend to move the workpiece in the direction the roller is facing. This means if it's not dead-on, it'll cause the workpiece to angle off to one side or the other. Second, a workpiece fed onto a roller will tend to roll away unassisted. Both problems are eliminated by replacing the roller with a pair of low-friction skids. And that's exactly what the folks at Triton have done (www.triton.net.au). Making their stand even better, the head of the stand has a built-in clamp and it swivels so it can be used for much more than outfeed support. And like all quality stands, the Triton folds up for compact storage.

3 Basic Table Saw Techniques

The table saw is the workhorse of most shops because it's the main tool used to prepare stock — that is, to break down large sheets of plywood into smaller pieces, to cut long boards into short lengths and wide boards into narrower pieces. And that's what this chapter is all about: the basics of using a table saw — everything from preparing and making rips and crosscuts to cutting miters and working with wide, long, narrow, and even irregular stock.

We'll show how to set up your rip fence and miter gauge to make accurate cuts, and explain a number of techniques you can use to cut plywood cleanly, support long or wide boards, and safely cut thin, narrow strips. There's even a section on positioning your saw in your shop for optimum performance, plus tips on how to safely cut non-wood materials like plastics and laminate.

Although ripping a board into narrower pieces may seem like a basic operation (and it is), there are a surprising number of tips and techniques you can learn that will make ripping safe and precise; ripping is just one of the many operations completely explained in this chapter.

Changing Blades

How easy it is to change a blade depends on a few things: how the throat plate is removed, how wide the throat opening is, and whether it requires one or two wrenches. The throat plate on a table saw fits into a recess in the top. Most plates provide some kind of spring detent that locks it in place; others require that you remove a set of screws.

The opening in the saw top is set by the manufacturer. Understandably, it needs to be as small as possible to prevent the top from warping, but more room to maneuver would be a plus. It can be downright uncomfortable at times trying to fit your hand plus a blade in the opening — particularly when installing dado sets. Most saws come with a single wrench, and you'll need to use a scrap of wood to keep the blade from spinning as the nut is loosened or tightened. Other manufacturers machine a flat on the arbor for a second wrench.

Removing a blade

To loosen an arbor nut using a single wrench and scrap block, slip the end of the scrap into a gullet between the teeth (mitering the end at 45 degrees makes this easier). Then with the wrench fitted on the arbor nut, pull the wrench toward you to loosen the nut (top photo). Spin the arbor nut off the arbor and carefully remove the stabilizer (if used), and then lift out the blade.

Installing a blade

When installing a blade, it's a good idea to develop this habit: Cup your hand under the blade (middle photo) as you lower it into the opening. This prevents the fragile carbide tips from accidentally chipping if they come in contact with the saw top. Although carbide is tough, it is brittle and chips easily if banged against metal.

Tightening an arbor nut

If you've ever dropped an arbor nut down into a saw cabinet, you'll appreciate this simple trick. As you remove or install the nut, slip it over your finger (inset below). Then press your fingertip against the arbor and slide the nut onto the arbor — simple and very effective. Once in place, tighten the nut by inserting your scrap block between the teeth at the rear of the blade as shown in the bottom photo. Then slip the wrench over the nut and away from you to tighten.

Bench Dog Blade-Loc

Want an alternative to using a scrap block to prevent the blade from spinning while tightening or loosening an arbor nut? Consider the Blade-Loc by Bench Dog (www.benchdog.com). The advantage this offers over a scrap block is that the saw teeth are completely covered by the Blade-Loc so there's no chance of injury from the wrench slipping and your hand making contact with the blade (left photo). To use the Blade-Loc, simply lower it onto the blade and tighten or loosen the arbor nut — the saw blade will be kept from spinning as soon as one of the plastic arms in the front and back of the Blade-Loc comes in contact with the saw top.

WORKING WITH DADO SETS

Most dado sets consist of an inner and outer blade and a set of chippers that you can insert between these to define the width of the dado. On some sets the outer and inner blade are interchangeable; on others they're not. Check the installation instructions on your dado set to see which kind you have.

Install the inner blade. If your dado set has an inner and outer blade, start by locating the inner blade. Drop it into the saw top opening and slide it onto the arbor (top photo at right).

Install the chippers. Now you can add the chippers. Most sets have four 1/8" chippers and a single 1/16" chipper. Mix and match for the desired width of the dado (middle photo at right). Most inner and outer blades cut 1/8" kerfs. Using just these produces a 1/4"-wide dado. If you need an odd-sized dado, use the shims that come with some sets and insert between the chippers. If your set doesn't have these shims, you can make your own from plastic laminate or thin metal or plastic.

Install the outer blade. All that's left is to slip on the outer blade, the stabilizer, and the arbor nut (bottom photo at right). If you're using all of the chippers, you may find that there's not enough room for both the stabilizer and the arbor nut. In cases like this, it's safest to set the stabilizer aside and thread the arbor nut fully onto the arbor before tightening.

Preparing to Make a Cut

With a saw blade installed, you may think you're ready to cut, but there are several steps still to take. Proper preparation is one of the keys to cutting safely and accurately on the table saw.

Marking and layout

For starters, it's always a good idea to mark the cut line on the workpiece you intend to cut. Take the time to do this right, using a try square or combination square as shown in the top photo. Mark both the face and the edge of the workpiece, and always mark an "X" to identify the waste side. You'll appreciate this if you get confused when cutting multiple pieces — and you'll save a lot of good wood from ending up in the scrap bin.

Hearing, eye, and dust protection

Any cut you make on the table saw will create sawdust. And there will always be a chance of kickback or a piece of wood being thrown in the air. That's why it's so important to protect yourself when sawing. Also, all table saws makes noise — those with universal motors tend to really whine — so keep a set of earmuffs within easy reach and wear them religiously. Other musts: eye protection and a dust mask to keep dust from entering your eyes and lungs (middle photo).

Dust collection

A dust mask will keep dust out of your lungs, but not out of the shop. We strongly recommend that you connect a shop vacuum or dust collection system to your saw whenever you use it, see the bottom photo. Most bench-top table saws (like the one shown in the bottom photo) have a convenient port in the rear that accepts the hose connector of the standard shop vacuum.

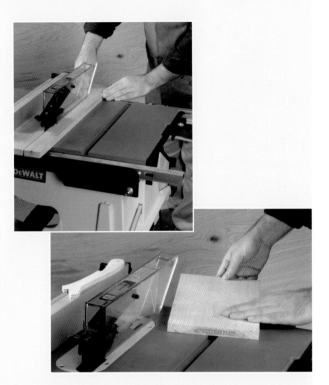

Proper stance

We can't overemphasize the importance of proper stance when using the table saw. As a general rule, position your body to either side of the cut (top photo). Which side depends on what side of the blade the rip fence is on, and whether you're right- or left-handed. The reason for this is that it prevents injury if kickback occurs. There are a number of causes of kickback, but they all result in the same thing — the workpiece is thrown violently backwards. If you're standing behind the blade, the impact can cause a serious injury.

Keep a push stick handy

Whether you think you'll need one or not, make it a habit to keep a push stick handy whenever you make a cut. Set one on your rip fence if it's wide enough or on the other side within easy reach. It's always safer to push a workpiece past a blade with a push stick than with your fingers. The push stick doesn't bleed if it contacts the spinning blade.

BLADE EXPOSURE RULES

There's been a lot of debate over the years on how much blade should be exposed when you make a cut. To keep saw blades running cool and to prevent burning, some saw manufacturers suggest that the blade be raised high enough so that the gullets between the teeth are completely exposed at the apex of the cut. This does allow the gullets to throw the dust from the blade. But it also exposes more blade than most safety folks are comfortable with. Going in the other direction, if the teeth just barely clear the workpiece, the teeth don't cut as cleanly (bottom drawing).

The generally accepted rule of thumb for blade exposure is to raise the blade so there's approximately 1/8" to 3/16" of the blade exposed at the apex (middle drawing). One way to adjust blade height quickly when using a carbide-tipped blade is to raise the blade until one full carbide tooth is exposed at the apex of the cut, see the photo above. This allows for chip clearance while also keeping a minimum of blade exposed.

HOW MUCH TO EXPOSE?

Blade Too High

Gullets Clear Workpiece

Blade Set for Optimum Waste Removal

Tip of Blade Approximately 1/8" above Surface

Safest Blade Height

Stock preparation

Since many operations at the table saw (ripping and crosscutting) have to do with stock preparation — that is, cutting parts to size for a project — consider building a rolling table like the one shown in the top photo. A table like this keeps the uncut and cut stock conveniently at hand. If you build the table so the top is slightly lower than the top of your table saw, you can even use it as an outfeed or side support when cutting long stock (for more on dealing with long stock, see page 49).

Blade storage

Another quick project you might want to consider building for your table saw is a simple blade storage unit like the one shown in the drawing below. This is nothing more than a plywood box with shelves spaced about $1/2"$ apart. Blade storage like this keeps your blades from coming in contact with one another, which can damage the teeth — especially brittle carbide teeth.

BLADE STORAGE

Rabbet Sides
to Accept Top
and Bottom

3/4" Plywood or
MDF Case

Groove or
Dado Sides
to Accept
Dividers

1/4" Dividers

Miter gauge holder

Since you'll be using your miter gauge a lot, you'll want some kind of holder for it to keep it within reach. Most bench-top saws, like the DeWalt shown in the bottom photo, have a built-in holder for the miter gauge. Most cabinet and contractor's saws don't provide storage, so you'll want to make a simple holder and attach it to the base of your saw or on a nearby wall. Two horizontal wood blocks spaced the width of the miter gauge bar apart work well for this. The bar is slipped between the blocks, and the head of the gauge rests on them with the bar pointing down, appearing much like a cross.

Setting blade height with a combination square

In many instances, you'll want to adjust the blade to a set height. For example, you might want to set it exactly 2" high to cut a tenon, or $5/8$" high to cut a groove. One way to measure blade height is to use a combination square as shown in the top photo. Adjust the blade of the square away from the head the desired depth of cut. Then simply place the blade end flat on the saw top and raise the blade until it just touches the square head.

Setting blade height using spacer blocks

Another option that's taken from machinists is to use calibrated spacer blocks. You can make a simple set by cutting like-sized pieces of $1/8$" and $1/4$" hardboard and $1/2$" and $3/4$" MDF (medium-density fiberboard). These engineered products are made with pretty tight tolerances. By mixing and matching these four blocks, you can easily set blade heights in $1/8$" increments. Say you want to set the blade for a $3/8$"-deep cut. Stack the $1/8$"-hardboard spacer on top of the $1/4$" spacer (to create a $3/8$"-thick block) and butt these up against the blade as shown in the photo below. Then raise the blade until the tips of the teeth are flush with the blocks at the apex of the cut.

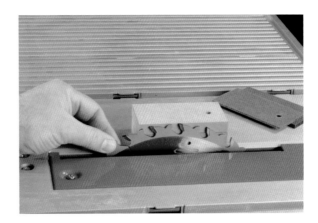

TABLE SAW SAFETY RULES

1 Read the instruction manual that came with your saw from cover to cover and follow all safety rules.

2 Use certified safety equipment: eye, hearing, and dust protection.

3 Dress properly: Don't wear ties, gloves, or loose clothing; remove all jewelry.

4 Never use a power saw in wet or damp locations.

5 Maintain your saw in peak condition; see Chapter 6 for more on this.

6 Before using your saw, check for damaged parts and make repairs as needed.

7 Keep your work area clean and uncluttered.

8 Keep children, pets, and visitors away when operating the saw.

9 Always use the guard and push sticks or push blocks whenever possible.

10 Listen to your "safety sense"; if a cut seems dangerous, it probably is. Stop and rethink the cut.

11 Never use force to make a cut. If force is needed, something is wrong. Stop the saw and find out what's not right.

12 Turn off the saw and unplug it before changing blades or accessories.

13 Never leave a saw running unattended; turn it off if you need to walk away from it.

14 Use dust collection whenever possible to protect your lungs and reduce dust in the shop.

15 Never reach around or over a spinning blade — this is one of the primary causes of saw-related injuries.

Splitter Guard Alignment

The number one safety device for your table saw is the splitter guard assembly. The splitter portion of this assembly is just a piece of sheet metal shaped to match the curve of your saw blade. It's positioned directly behind the blade to separate or "split" the piece you're cutting in two. It also helps prevent binding if the kerf was too close due to casehardening (see page 157 for more on this). Attached to the splitter are a pair of barbed anti-kickback pawls, designed to allow the workpiece and waste piece to pass in one direction only. If kickback were to occur, the pointed barbs of the pawls should bite into the wood, preventing it from being thrown back toward the operator. At the very end of the assembly is a hinged, clear plastic guard that rests on top of the blade. This guard serves both to keep your fingers away from the spinning blade and also to prevent wood chips and splinters from being thrown out toward you.

Alignment with the blade
For the splitter assembly to work correctly, it must be aligned with the blade. The easiest way to check this is to butt a straightedge up against the saw blade as shown in the top photo.

Adjusting the splitter
The splitter assembly should be flush with or slightly back from the straightedge. If it isn't, you'll need to adjust it. How you adjust a splitter assembly will depend on the table saw. Some versions attach directly behind the blade inside the cabinet and are adjusted from side to side by adding or removing shims. On most contractor and cabinet saws, the splitter attaches to the trunion behind the saw table as shown in the middle photo. Some saws (like the one shown here) use a convenient sliding plate; all you need do is loosen the connecting bolts and slide the plate side to side to align it with the blade.

Checking anti-kickback pawls
Just because a splitter guard assembly has anti-kickback pawls doesn't mean they'll work when you need

them. It's a good idea to regularly check them to make sure they're working. A simple way to do this is to slide a long scrap of wood past one pawl at a time as shown in the bottom photo. Then grip the scrap and try to pull it back toward the front of the saw. The teeth of the pawl should sink into the scrap, preventing it from moving backwards. If they don't, the barbs of the pawl are most likely dull and need to be sharpened (see page 45 for how to do this). Repeat this procedure for the remaining pawl.

Sharpening anti-kickback pawls

When anti-kickback pawls don't bite into wood, the barbs are probably dull. To sharpen them, use a slim taper file like the one shown in the top photo to sharpen each tooth. Sharpen the inside edge of the tooth as shown in the top photo until a sharp point is formed. After you've sharpened all the teeth of both pawls, check each one with the long scrap as you did in the previous step.

Checking the guard

Every time you get ready to make a cut, you should check your saw guard to make sure it's functioning properly. This takes only a few seconds and is well worth the time. Simply grab the top of the saw guard as shown in the middle photo and lift it up. Then wiggle it to make sure it pivots at the back where it attaches to the splitter assembly and at the top where it attaches to the guard bracket. Doing this ensures that there are no obstructions that will prevent the guard from rising as the workpiece is cut and riding along its top. It's easy for a small scrap of wood to catch in either pivot point and keep the guard from working properly.

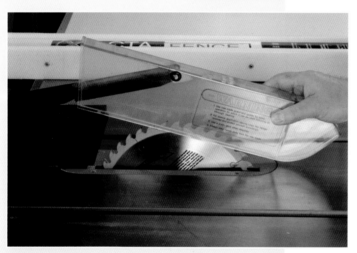

Cleaning the guard

The clear plastic portion of your table saw guard will quickly become opaque as a film of sawdust builds up inside from cutting stock. Anytime you notice a buildup, stop and clean the guard. The quickest way to do this is with a can of compressed air. Just lift the guard and give it a couple of shots of air inside, see the bottom photo. Blowing off the dust like this is better than wiping it off. Wiping tends to create tiny scratches in the plastic that over time will make the plastic less transparent.

Saw Location in the Shop

Where you locate the table saw in your shop will have a major impact on its ease of use. The more you know about necessary clearances and workflow, the better you'll be able to position the saw for optimum performance (see below). Additionally, you can improve performance in a tight space by positioning other tools nearby to serve as support (see the opposite page).

Table saw clearances

To make cuts on standard stock, including full sheets of plywood, you'll need to locate the saw as shown in the top drawing. Unfortunately, this isn't possible in all shops, so you'll have to do the best you can. One way to maximize a small space is to position the saw at an angle so that you use the longer diagonal distance in your space. Keeping your table saw on a mobile base (see page 30) will give you greater flexibility in shop layout.

Workflow in the shop

The bottom drawing illustrates typical workflow in the shop. Lumber is brought into the shop and stored in racks. When it's time to build a project, lumber is removed and broken down at the table and is planed if necessary, and the edges are jointed. All this takes place in the stock preparation area, so it makes sense to group these tools together. Once the stock is prepped, it moves on to the hand and power tool work area.

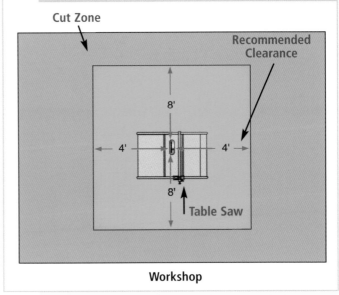

TABLE SAW CLEARANCES

Cut Zone

Recommended Clearance

8'

4'   4'

8'

Table Saw

Workshop

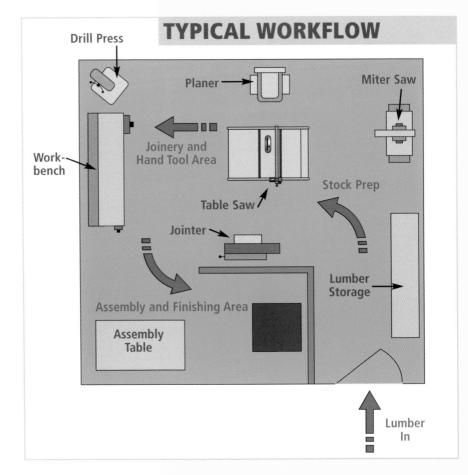

TYPICAL WORKFLOW

Drill Press

Planer

Miter Saw

Work-bench

Joinery and Hand Tool Area

Stock Prep

Table Saw

Jointer

Lumber Storage

Assembly and Finishing Area

Assembly Table

Lumber In

OUTFEED SUPPORT FROM A ROUTER TABLE

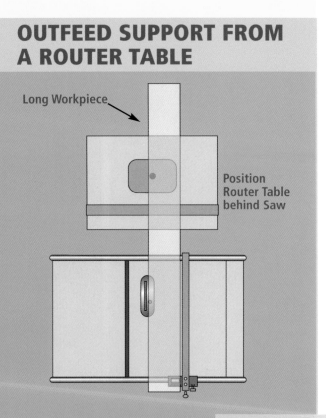

Long Workpiece

Position Router Table behind Saw

Front of Table Saw

Outfeed support

In shops short on space, you can group your tools to create support for table saw cuts. Positioning a router table directly behind the table saw as shown in the top drawing is an excellent way to create outfeed support. For this to work, however, the top of the router table should be approximately $1/4$" lower than the top of the table saw. This will allow a workpiece to slide onto the table without catching on the front edge. A shaper with a removable fence will also work fine here.

Side support

When you're crosscutting long boards, it's good to have some kind of side support to prevent the board from bowing. An easy way to have this support all the time is to position your workbench to the side of the table saw, as shown in the bottom drawing. Here again, the workbench will need to be about $1/4$" to $1/2$" lower than the top of the table saw to prevent it from catching the end of the workpiece. An assembly table or storage cart can also be used for this.

SIDE SUPPORT FROM A WORKBENCH

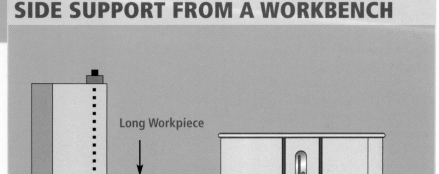

Long Workpiece

Miter Gauge

Table Saw

Position Workbench to Side of Saw

Ripping

Ripping stock to width along its grain is one of the most basic operations you can do on a table saw. It's something you'll do for virtually every project you make. Although standard ripping is pretty straight-forward, there are some tricks involved in ripping long and wide stock (page 49), narrow stock (page 50), thick stock (page 51), plywood (page 52), and irregular stock where the edges are uneven (page 53), as well as ripping at an angle (page 54).

Check fence alignment

Before you make any rip cut, it's a good idea to check the rip fence for proper alignment. When a rip fence is properly aligned, it's parallel to the saw blade (or offset slightly, see page 146). If everything is aligned correctly on your table saw, the saw blade (and trunion) will be parallel to the miter gauge slot. (For more on checking and aligning the trunion, see pages 141–144.) This means you can check rip fence alignment by simply sliding the fence over until one edge is aligned with one side of the miter gauge slot. Lock the rip fence in place and gently run your finger along the inside edge of the miter gauge slot as shown in the top photo. The edge of the fence and the side of the slot should be aligned; if they're not, adjust the fence as described on page 147.

Set the rip fence

Once you're sure the rip fence is aligned, you can set it for the desired cut. There are two ways to do this. One is to rely on the built-in measure on the rip fence rail (if applicable). This works fine for rough positioning, but most seasoned wood-workers still use a tape measure or rule (middle photo). Why? The built-in indicator is reliable only for the blade it was calibrated for. Since blades vary in thickness, it can be off if you change blades.

Make the cut

With the rip fence set for the desired width, you can make your cut, as in the bottom photo.

Whenever possible, use a push stick to feed the workpiece past the blade. If you do push with just your hands, wrap the finger of your right hand over the fence as you push the workpiece. This simple precaution can prevent your hand from being pulled into the saw blade if your fingers come in contact with the blade.

Long stock support

Anytime you need to rip stock that's longer than one-half the depth (width) of your table saw, you should set up some kind of support on the outfeed side of the table to catch and support the workpiece as you finish the cut, see the top photo. Supports with rollers are common, but they tend to skew the workpiece to one side or another if not perfectly parallel to the back edge of the saw. Supports with curved plastic tops like the Triton multi-stand (www.triton.net.au) shown in the photo provide the necessary support without skewing the workpiece.

Add an outrigger

Another way to provide support when ripping long boards is to make a simple outrigger and attach it to your rip fence, see the middle photo. The outrigger is nothing more than a long board with a pair of shorter supports glued and screwed perpendicular to the ends to form L-shapes on the infeed and outfeed side of the saw. This simple jig does a great job of supporting most long stock.

RIPPING WIDE STOCK

Wide stock can be a challenge to rip because it's heavier and the weight tends to pull the workpiece away from the rip fence when cutting. Here are two ways you can prevent that from happening: Use an extended fence, and replace the fence with a clamped-on cleat.

Extend the fence. Attaching a long auxiliary fence to your rip fence provides more stable starting and stopping points for cutting a wide workpiece.

Replace the fence with a cleat. Another way to handle a wide rip is to clamp a cleat under the edge of the workpiece as shown to cut to the desired width. Butt the cleat against the side of the saw table and push to make the cut.

Compound Cuts

When you make a bevel cut and a miter cut in the same operation, it's called a compound cut. To do this, you tilt both the blade and the miter gauge to create a shape with tapered, tilted sides. Picture frames are often joined together with compound cuts. Crown molding is another example.

Although the premise is simple, there are two things that make compound cuts a challenge. First, there are no preset stops on either the miter gauge or blade tilt for most of the angles you'll need. Second, it's difficult to keep a mental image of the finished project with respect to the cuts you're making. This is particularly true for crown molding. The trick is to think of the saw table as the ceiling. And imagine the room upside down and the fence corresponding to the wall.

Adjusting both the miter gauge and the fence is easier with an adjustable protractor. Even with this, it's important that you make sets of test cuts on scraps to make sure the angles are correct. For example, if you're making an apple tray with 4"-wide tilted sides, make a couple of sets of 4"-wide scraps. Cut all four sides, test the fit, and adjust as necessary. When the joints are perfect, cut your project stock.

Angle blade and miter gauge
To make a compound cut, start by angling the blade (see the chart). Make a test cut and check with a protractor. Then adjust the miter gauge, make a test cut, and check this with a protractor (inset).

Make the cut
Once the blade and miter gauge are tilted to the correct angles, make a set of test cuts on a piece of scrap. Check the fit and adjust either or both angles as necessary and try again. Fine-tuning is really a matter of trial and error.

ANGLES FOR COMMON COMPOUND CUTS

Pitch of Sides		Four Sides	Six Sides	Eight Sides
0 degrees	Miter angle	45.0 degrees	30.0 degrees	22.5 degrees
15 degrees	Miter angle	44.0 degrees	29.1 degrees	21.8 degrees
	Bevel angle*	79.5 degrees	82.6 degrees	84.3 degrees
30 degrees	Miter angle	40.9 degrees	26.6 degrees	19.7 degrees
	Bevel angle*	69.3 degrees	75.5 degrees	79.0 degrees
45 degrees	Miter angle	35.3 degrees	22.2 degrees	16.3 degrees
	Bevel angle*	60.0 degrees	69.3 degrees	74.3 degrees
60 degrees	Miter angle	26.6 degrees	16.1 degrees	11.7 degrees
	Bevel angle*	52.2 degrees	64.3 degrees	70.6 degrees
75 degrees	Miter angle	14.5 degrees	8.5 degrees	6.1 degrees
	Bevel angle*	46.9 degrees	61.1 degrees	68.3 degrees
90 degrees	Bevel angle*	45.0 degrees	60.0 degrees	67.5 degrees

*Bevel angle given is angle between saw blade and table top, NOT the tilt as shown on the saw's tilt scale.

Narrow Stock

Many woodworking projects call for thin strips or slats — a tambour desktop, for instance, or splines for a mitered spline joint (see page 76). The problem with ripping narrow strips is twofold: It's difficult and dangerous to rip with the rip fence close to the blade — you can't safely get a push stick in place to move the strip past the blade; also, thin strips can and will fall into the normal opening in the throat plate. The way to get around these problems and cut narrow stock safely is to use a notched sled to push the workpiece past the blade (see below), and a zero-clearance insert to keep the strips from falling into the opening in the throat plate (see the sidebar).

Notched sled

A notched sled can be made two ways: Cut a notch in the side of a piece of scrap wood (see the drawing at right), or glue a short scrap of wood to the side of scrap wood to serve as a lip to catch and push the workpiece forward. To use the notched sled, adjust the rip fence and sled to cut the desired thickness strip. Then insert your workpiece into the notch, turn on the saw, and push the sled and workpiece past the blade, see the photo above. Remove the strip from the sled, reinsert the workpiece, and continue cutting as many strips as you need. The beauty of this setup is that you don't have to adjust the rip fence after each cut, and all the strips will be of uniform thickness.

NOTCHED SLED FOR CUTTING NARROW STOCK

Narrow Strip

← Feed

Blank

ZERO-CLEARANCE INSERT

A zero-clearance insert is a special shop-made insert that hugs the blade and prevents thin strips from dropping down into the normal wider blade slot, see the photo at right. A built-in splitter also helps prevent binding, see the drawing below.

INSERT WITH BUILT-IN SPLITTER

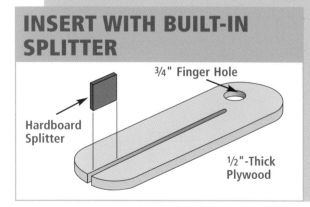

3/4" Finger Hole

Hardboard Splitter

1/2"-Thick Plywood

You can use your standard throat plate as a template to make a zero-clearance insert. First, place the throat plate on a 1/2"-thick piece of plywood and trace around it. Then cut it to rough shape to within 1/8" of the outline. Next, temporarily attach the throat plate to the plywood with double-sided tape. Now you can trim it to exact size with a flush-trim bit in a router. Drill a 3/4" finger hole in the insert, and cut a kerf in it for a splitter that aligns with the blade. Glue a 1/8" piece of hardboard in the end of the kerf, and you're ready to rip narrow stock safely.

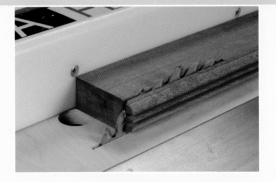

Narrow molding

Another instance where you'll often need to rip narrow stock is when making moldings. Here's the safest way to do it. Start by shaping the edges of the molding as desired on the edge of your workpiece. Then cut a pair of grooves in the edge of the workpiece to define the width of the molding, see the drawing at left. This way you can rip the narrow strips off safely as shown in the top photo.

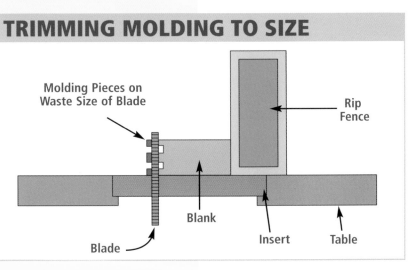

TRIMMING MOLDING TO SIZE

Molding Pieces on Waste Size of Blade

Rip Fence

Blank

Insert

Table

Blade

RIPPING THICK STOCK

Stock that's thicker than the maximum cut on your table saw can usually be ripped by taking two passes. An operation similar to this is resawing; see pages 68–69 for more on this.

Take the first pass. Set the rip fence for the desired width and raise the blade to roughly one-half the thickness of the workpiece. Hook up dust collection, since ripping thick stock produces a lot of dust. Turn on the saw and, keeping the workpiece pressed firmly against the fence, push it past the blade. Use a push stick, see the top photo at right.

Make a second pass. Now flip the workpiece end for end, taking care to keep the same side against the rip fence — it's a good idea to mark your reference side with an "X" to avoid confusion. Turn on the saw and, using a push stick, feed the workpiece past the blade to cut the piece in half, see the bottom photo at right.

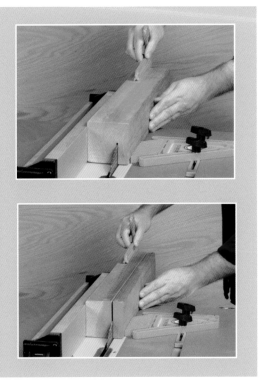

Plywood

Because it's constructed of several thin layers of veneer (called plies), plywood can be a challenge to cut smoothly with a table saw. Even if you use a plywood blade with many small teeth, the thin outer layer (or face veneer) can and will tear. Fortunately, there are a number of simple tricks you can use to control tear-out.

Cut with the good face up

For starters, tear-out isn't a problem if only the "good" or show face of the plywood will be seen. So all you have to do is protect the good face. Do this by placing the good face up when cutting on the table saw, see the top photo. This won't prevent splintering — it still occurs, but only on the unseen face.

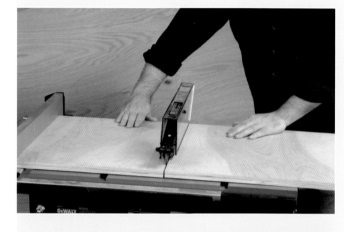

Score the face veneer first

When both faces of the plywood will be seen, there are a couple of tricks you can use to reduce splintering. One way to prevent tear-out is to sever the wood fibers in advance — this way they can't tear out. Start by marking the cut line on the good face of your plywood. Then, using a metal straightedge and sharp knife, cut cleanly along the marked line as shown in the middle photo. Cutting about $1/16$" deep will suffice, as it's the surface veneer that has the greatest tendency to tear out.

Support the veneer with tape

Another trick is to cover the cut line on both sides with masking tape; the tape helps keep the thin veneer from chipping out during the cut, see the bottom photo. Finally, consider using the double-cut technique. Set your saw blade to cut about three-quarters of the way through the plywood, and make a cut. Then, simply flip the plywood over and make another pass to complete the cut. The finished edge should be virtually chip-free.

RIPPING IRREGULAR STOCK

Occasionally, you'll need to rip a board that has uneven edges. If you purchase lumber from a sawmill, this may be a frequent problem unless you pay to have the stock straight-line ripped. There are two ways to rip wood like this: Use a sled, or tack on a straight reference edge.

A ripping sled. A sled used to rip irregular stock is nothing more than a piece of scrap plywood that's a bit wider than the stock you need to rip, see the drawing at right. The workpiece is attached to the sled with screws, double-sided tape, or simple lever-style clamps as shown in the top photo. Angle the workpiece on the sled as needed to position the entire uneven edge over the edge of the sled nearest the blade. Then adjust the rip fence away from the blade the width of the sled. Turn on the saw and push the sled past the blade to cut a perfect straight edge. Remove the workpiece from the sled, place the straight edge against the fence, and rip it to the desired width.

STRAIGHT-LINE RIPPING JIG

Screw Board to Plywood Carriage

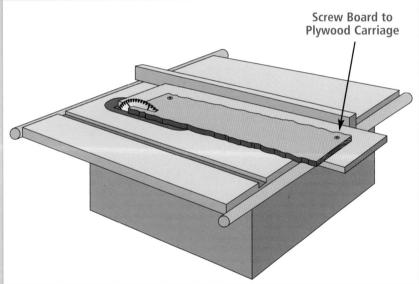

Tacked-on straightedge. Another way to handle uneven edges is to attach a straight-edged scrap on top of the workpiece to be cut (bottom photo). This way you can butt the straight edge of the scrap against the rip fence to cut a straight edge on the workpiece. Attach the scrap with nails, screws, or double-sided tape.

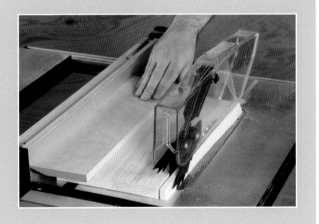

Ripping at an Angle

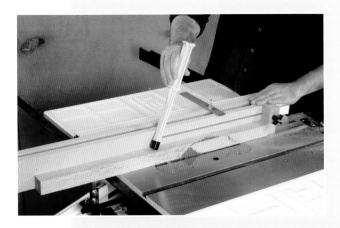

Some projects require you to rip stock at an angle. These angled cuts may be from end to end on a workpiece to create a tapered leg (for an example of tapered legs, see pages 160–164), or the angle can be from face to face on a board, such as when bevel-ripping to join pieces at an angle (for an example of joining bevel-ripped parts, see the blanket chest on pages 170–175).

Use a taper jig

One way to rip parts at an angle from end to end is to use a taper jig, like the one shown in the top photo. The jig holds the piece in place and adjusts for the desired angle. The jig and workpiece slide along the rip fence as they're pushed forward past the blade. Taper jigs can be purchased or made in the shop. Plans for the shop-made jig shown here are on pages 126–129).

Use a notched sled

Another way to rip a workpiece at an angle from end to end is to use a notched sled (middle photo). This is simply a scrap of plywood that you notch at the desired angle to cradle the workpiece. Insert the piece to be cut in the notch and adjust the rip fence for the desired cut. Then just turn on the saw and, with the side of the sled pressed up against the rip fence, push the sled past the blade. The workpiece will be cut at the desired angle, and you can repeat this process for additional parts as needed without having to readjust the rip fence.

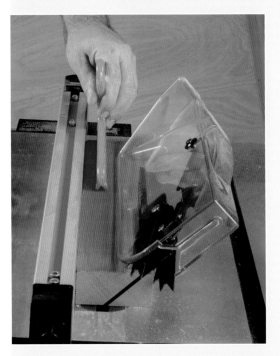

Bevel-ripping

When you need to cut a workpiece at an angle from face to face — a bevel rip — all you need to do is tilt the blade to the desired angle, set the rip fence for the desired width of cut, and push the workpiece past the blade, see the bottom photo. Make sure to check the guard for proper operation before making the cut: Tilting the blade often causes it to bind against the saw top.

Crosscutting

Next to ripping, crosscutting stock to length against the grain is second most common table saw operation. Generally, longer boards are broken down into shorter lengths. The workpiece is pushed past the blade with the miter gauge that fits in the slot or track cut into the saw top.

Miter gauge setup

The key to precision crosscuts is a miter gauge that's perfectly perpendicular to the blade. Before you adjust the miter gauge, though, make sure that the saw blade and its carriage — the trunion — are parallel to the miter gauge slot (see page 142). If it's not parallel, you'll need to adjust the trunion; see pages 141–145. Once it's aligned, you can adjust the miter gauge. A simple way to do this is to place the head of a try or framing square against the head of the miter gauge and slide it over so the blade of the square butts up against the saw blade, see the top photo. Rotate the saw blade as necessary so the square blade rests flat on the blade and not on the teeth. Loosen the miter gauge lock and pivot it as necessary to bring the square blade perfectly flush against the saw blade; then tighten the miter gauge lock.

Attach an auxiliary fence

The heads of miter gauges are quite short (typically 5" to 7"). This does not provide adequate support for most cuts. To better support a workpiece, attach a wood auxiliary fence to the body of the miter gauge (middle photo). There are holes in the body of the miter gauge just for this purpose. If you extend the fence an inch or two past the saw blade, it will also support the cutoff and prevent tear-out.

Use sandpaper to prevent creep

To prevent your workpiece from "creeping" or shifting during the cut, apply a piece of sandpaper to the face of the auxiliary fence, see the bottom photo. The grit of the paper will help grip the workpiece. Creep is caused by blades that are improperly sharpened or set incorrectly. Set is usually a problem only on a non-carbide-tipped blade. Here, alternate teeth are bent or set slightly to create a wider kerf so the blade won't bind during a cut. When the set on one side of the teeth is too heavy, the blade tends to pull or push a workpiece during a cut, much like the "drift" problems associated with band saws.

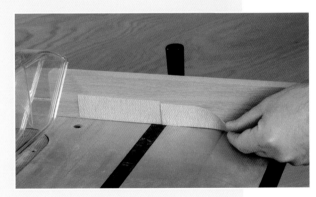

Use a stop block

For super-accurate crosscuts, it's best to clamp a stop block to the auxiliary fence as shown in the top photo. Not only does this guarantee the workpiece will be cut the correct width, but it also makes it extremely easy to duplicate parts. To position the stop block, measure from the saw blade over to the desired length. Then clamp the block in place. Double-check your setup by measuring from the stop block back to the saw blade, and adjust as necessary. When it looks good, gently butt your workpiece up against the stop block. With the side edge of the workpiece flat against the auxiliary fence, push the workpiece past the blade to cut it to length.

Stop block sawdust relief

When using a stop block, you may find that sawdust builds up near the block. This can affect the accuracy of the cut if the dust gets between the stop block and the end of the workpiece. To prevent this, make a small miter cut on the bottom corner of the stop block as shown in the middle photo. The relief cut provides a channel for sawdust to flow through so that it can't build up and mess up your cut.

Ganged cuts for efficiency

If you find that you need to crosscut a set of parts to identical length, consider making a ganged cut. Basically, all you're doing with a ganged cut is stacking a couple of parts on top of each other and cutting them simultaneously in groups, see the bottom photo. The only thing you'll have to be careful of here is to make sure that your saw blade is perfectly perpendicular to the saw table. Otherwise, the ends of the top workpieces could end up with a slight angle.

Crosscutting wide panels

Some projects may call for crosscutting a wide workpiece. This is where a table saw fitted with a sliding table comes in particularly handy, see the top photo. If you don't have a sliding table, you can safely crosscut wide pieces by using the clamp-on cleat technique described on the bottom of page 49.

Crosscutting short pieces

Crosscutting short pieces can be dangerous on the table saw. First, since the head of the miter gauge is so short, the piece may not be properly supported. So the first thing you should do is attach an auxiliary fence as described on page 55. It's also a good idea to attach sandpaper to the fence to prevent the short piece from shifting during the cut (and use a stop block). Second, your hands end up too close to the blade. The safest way to crosscut a short piece is to clamp it in place to keep your hands far from the spinning blade. That's where specialty miter gauges with built-in hold-downs (like the one shown in the middle photo) really shine. If you don't have one of these, press the workpiece into the miter gauge bar with a push stick like the yellow one shown in the top photo on page 33. This will help keep the piece from shifting during the cut.

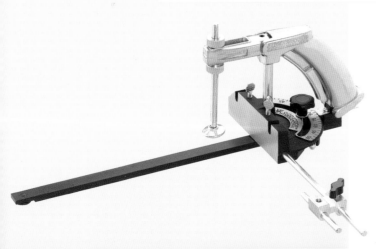

Beveled crosscuts

Whenever you need to crosscut at an angle — that is, when the saw blade is angled away from perpendicular — make sure to move the miter gauge into the slot that will allow you to make the cut so the blade is angled away from your hands, as shown in the bottom photo. It just makes good safety sense to keep the teeth as far away from your hands as possible. This also generally results in a cleaner cut with less burning. The workpiece isn't pinched between the saw blade and saw top as it would be if you cut with the blade angled toward your hand.

Cutting Miters

Angled crosscuts — miters — are commonly cut on the table saw. Basically, the miter gauge is set to the desired angle and the cut is made similar to a regular crosscut. The only differences are that it can be difficult to set the angle correctly and that, since the miter gauge is angled, the workpiece will tend to shift away from the cut.

Adjusting the miter gauge

Setting the angle of a miter gauge can be tricky because there are usually only three set stops: 90 degrees, and 45 degrees in each direction. Any other degree cut must be set up with trial and error. To set up a 45-degree cut, consider using a speed square as shown in the top photo. Loosen the miter lock and pivot the head so a speed square butted against the miter head is perfectly flush with the saw blade. Then tighten the lock (see pages 148–149 for tips on maintaining your miter gauge). Angles other than 45 degrees are best set by using an adjustable protractor, taking a test cut, and measuring and adjusting the miter gauge as needed.

Adding an auxiliary fence

Using an auxiliary fence is even more important for cutting miters than it is for standard crosscuts. The reason: Stops are vital to prevent the workpiece from shifting during the cut, and odds are you'll need the fence to attach a stop (middle photo). Before you add the fence, adjust the miter gauge to the desired angle and roughly calculate the length of the fence needed — you may be surprised how long it needs to be because of the angle. Add about 4" to this length for the stop block and to let the fence extend past the blade. This will help prevent tear-out as the blade exits the workpiece and will also allow you to safely push the waste piece past the blade.

Sandpaper to prevent creep

Just as you did for the fence when crosscutting, it's a good idea to apply a couple of strips of self-stick sandpaper to the face of the auxiliary fence (see the bottom photo). Do this even if you use a stop, because the blade may try to pull the workpiece into the blade as it cuts and the sandpaper will help prevent this. A stop block will help only if the blade tries to push the workpiece away from the blade.

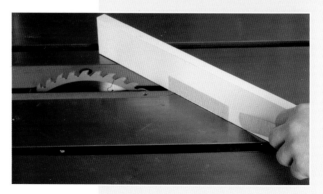

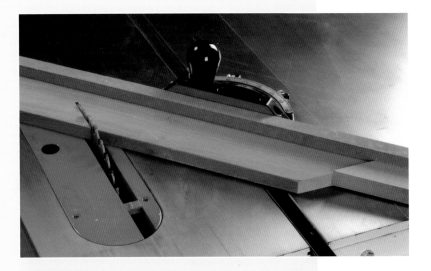

Consider using a mitered stop

To help hold a workpiece in place for mitering, it's best to use a stop block like the one described on page 56. If both ends of the workpiece are to be mitered, consider using a mitered stop block like the one shown in the photo at left. Mitering the block helps lock the workpiece in place better then a standard stop block, which can have trouble keeping the mitered end in place. You can clamp the mitered stop block in place or attach it with screws (as shown here).

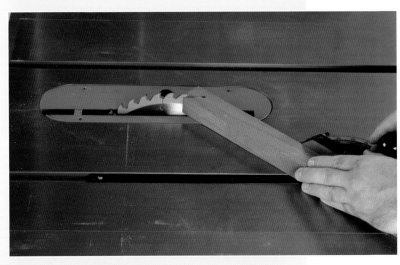

Open position

Whenever you want to miter the end of a workpiece, you're faced with a decision: Which way should I angle the miter gauge — to the left or to the right? When the miter gauge is pivoted to the left as shown in the middle photo, this is called the open position. Although this is the safest position (it keeps the operator's hands the farthest from the blade), many woodworkers feel it's awkward to miter like this. The big advantage to this position is that the cutting forces of the blade tend to push the workpiece back into the stop block, ensuring an accurate length. Additionally, the miter gauge bar and stock will remain fully supported at the end of the cut.

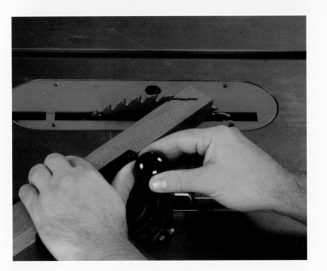

Closed position

When you pivot the head of the miter gauge to the right as shown in the bottom photo, the miter gauge is said to be in the closed position. Although a fairly natural position for most woodworkers, this position has a number of disadvantages. First, your hands are positioned too close to the blade. Second, the cutting forces of the blade tend to pull the work-piece away from the stop block, resulting in inaccurate cuts. And third, at the end of the cut the miter gauge tends to run out of slot, and the workpiece can wiggle without support.

MITERING WITH A SLED

Another way to cut accurate miters on the table saw is to replace the miter gauge with a miter sled. The sled is just a piece of plywood or MDF with runners in it that ride in the miter gauge slots. Angled cleats attached to the top serve as rests to hold your workpiece.

Make the base. The base of the miter sled shown here is 14" × 24". Center the base on the saw blade and mark the miter gauge slot locations on the edge of the base. Install a dado set in your saw and cut a pair of ³⁄₈"-deep channels to accept runners cut to fit your miter gauge slots, see the top photo. (For more on grooves and dadoes, see Chapter 4.)

Add the runners. Once the channels are cut on the underside of the sled base, cut a pair of runners from a sturdy hardwood such as oak or a high-grade plastic such as UHMW (ultra-high molecular weight) as described on page 61. Cut these to fit the slots and to thickness to fit into the channels in the sled base. Attach the runners with glue and allow them to dry overnight, see the middle photo above .

Attach the cleats. Cut a pair of cleats to width (ours are 2" wide) and attach them to the sled base with glue and screws. Turn on the saw and slide the sled forward until the saw cuts a kerf about halfway through the sled; use this kerf as reference when installing the cleats. Use a speed square or other reliable layout tool to position cleats exactly 45 degrees to the saw kerf as shown in the photo at right. Position the cleat about 4" back from the leading edge of the sled to allow space for your workpiece.

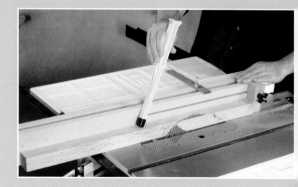

Miter your workpiece. To use the sled, butt your workpiece against the desired cleat and raise the saw blade up so it'll cut through the sled and the workpiece. Turn on the saw and push the sled and workpiece past the blade to make your cut, as shown in the bottom photo; take care to stop all forward motion as soon as the workpiece is cut to prevent cutting the sled in half.

CUTTING NON-WOOD MATERIALS

Plastics are becoming increasingly common in the woodshop. Unlike wood, which swells and shrinks as the humidity changes, plastic is dimensionally stable. This makes it perfect for making jigs and fixtures for the shop, where precision is paramount. The different types of plastic offer additional benefits. Clear plastics like acrylic are perfect for saw guards, as they let you see what you're cutting. Other plastics, like UHMW (ultra-high molecular weight), offer hard surfaces that are slick. These are excellent for use as a fence face where workpieces are constantly being pressed along the surface, or for parts that take a lot of abuse, like the runners on a sliding table. And tough plastic laminates are widely used to cover work surfaces, jigs, and fixtures in the shop.

Cutting plastic. Most plastics such as Lexan, Plexiglas, and acrylic can be cut quite satisfactorily on a table saw fitted with a carbide-tipped blade. The only thing to keep in mind (especially when cutting clear plastics like Plexiglas) is to use a feed rate that's slightly faster than you'd use when ripping wood, see the top photo. The reason for this is that slower feed rates create friction and the plastic will melt and not cut.

Cutting plastic laminate. Because plastic laminate is so thin — typically about 1/16" thick — it can be a tricky to cut on most table saws. The challenge is keeping the thin laminate from slipping under your rip fence. The best way to get around this is to make a special laminate-cutting fence that attaches to your rip fence, see the middle photo.

Laminate-cutting fence. In addition to keeping the laminate from slipping under your rip fence, the shop-made fence illustrated in the drawing below also has a built-in hold-down to keep the laminate from flexing up and ruining the cut. The fence is just a length of scrap cut to fit your fence. A kerf is cut in it to accept 1/8" or 1/4" hardboard that serves as the hold-down. A strip of plastic laminate is screwed to the bottom of the fence strip to keep the laminate being cut from slipping under the rip fence. In use, the fence is attached to your rip fence and adjusted for the desired width of cut.

The laminate to be cut is inserted between the hold-down and laminate strip attached to the bottom of the fence and pushed forward to make the cut.

FENCE HOLD-DOWN FOR LAMINATES

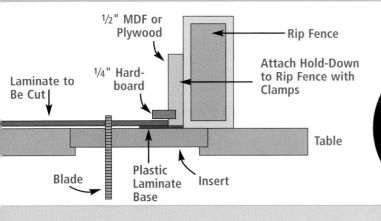

- 1/2" MDF or Plywood
- Rip Fence
- Attach Hold-Down to Rip Fence with Clamps
- 1/4" Hardboard
- Laminate to Be Cut
- Table
- Blade
- Plastic Laminate Base
- Insert

4 Advanced Table Saw Techniques

Although the table saw is used by most woodworkers as the primary tool for cutting lumber and sheet stock to size for projects, many ignore its joint-making capabilities. With the addition of just a dado set, the table saw can cut dadoes, grooves and rabbets, box joints, tenons — even faux mortises. What's more, you can make your own custom cove molding, resaw lumber, create sturdy frame-and-panel assemblies with flat or raised panels, curve wood, and even joint with the table saw.

Many of these techniques can be accomplished with just your standard table saw accessories, such as the miter gauge, rip fence, and saw blade. Others require building a jig. The simpler jigs are included in this chapter; more-advanced jigs are detailed in Chapter 5 on pages 96–129. Consider building one or more of these to make your table saw even more versatile than it already is.

The simple tenoning jig shown here is just one of the many easy-to-make jigs featured in this chapter that will let you exploit the joint-making capabilities of your table saw. This jig slips over and rides along your rip fence to accurately cut tenons on the end of a project part.

Stopped Cuts

Occasionally a project will call for a part with a stopped cut — that is, a cut that does not continue through the piece. This is the same as a plunge cut with a circular saw except that instead of lowering the blade into the workpiece, here you lower the workpiece into the blade. Stopped cuts are most often used for cutting a slot or cutouts in a workpiece when making jigs. Additionally, stopped cuts are useful for making L-shaped parts when there's no band saw in the shop.

Using stops

Stopped cuts are made by attaching one or two stops temporarily to the rip fence to define the starting and/or stopping points of the cut (right photo). If you're making an L-shaped part, you'll use one stop; two stops are needed for a slot or cutout within the workpiece. Secure the stop or stops to the rip fence with screw clamps — don't rely on spring clamps here since they can easily shift in use.

Vertical cuts

Because you're making a stopped cut with a round blade, the kerf at the end of the cut will be curved.

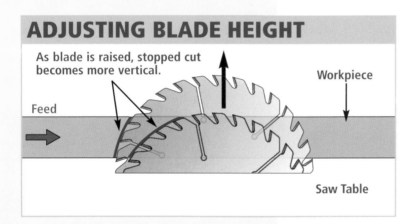

ADJUSTING BLADE HEIGHT

As blade is raised, stopped cut becomes more vertical.

Feed

Workpiece

Saw Table

This may or may not be an issue. If it is, consider raising the blade to its full height. Doing so makes the kerf as vertical as possible, as shown in the drawing at left. The downside to this is that you'll have a lot of blade exposed since the splitter/guard has to be removed for a stopped cut. If you decide to use this technique, make sure that the rip fence is aligned properly (see page 146) and that your blade is clean and sharp.

Lowering/raising the workpiece

If a raised blade makes you nervous, lower it so it just cuts through the workpiece. Then position one end of the workpiece up against the stop you set earlier. Now while keeping a firm grip on the workpiece and pressing it firmly against the rip fence, slowly lower it down onto the blade (bottom photo). Once it's flat on the table top, push the workpiece through the cut as you would any other. If both ends of the cut are stopped, you'll need to gently raise the workpiece off the blade when it hits the other stop. Alternatively, you can turn off the saw and remove the workpiece once the blade stops spinning.

Cutting Coves

Although you can purchase ready-made cove molding at most home centers, your choice of materials (usually pine, extruded foam, or red oak) and sizes and shapes is severely limited. So when a project calls for a unique coved part made of walnut or mahogany, you'll need to make the cove yourself. Fortunately, this is a fairly straightforward operation for the table saw. The secret to cutting coves on the table saw is to angle an auxiliary rip fence so it's not parallel to the blade and will make a scooped cut. The only tricky part is setting up the fence angle.

Define the cove
To determine the angle for the auxiliary fence, you'll need to first lay out the desired cove on a scrap cut to the same dimensions as your finished workpiece, see the top right drawing. Carefully mark both the width and the depth of the cove to be cut.

Make an alignment jig
The next step toward positioning the auxiliary fence is to make a simple alignment jig from scraps of thin wood or cardboard, see the middle drawing at right. Tape or staple together the strips of wood so that the long strips are separated by the width of the desired cove.

Set the angle
Raise the blade to the full height of the finished cove and set the alignment jig over the blade. Rotate the jig until the inside edges of the strips contact just the very tips of the blade. Then use a pencil to mark a line on the saw top along the inner edge of the near strip, as shown in the bottom photo. (If you don't want to mark your table top, first lay down a strip of masking tape to draw on or just use masking tape to mark the angle.)

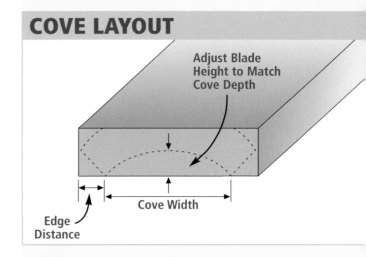

COVE LAYOUT

Adjust Blade Height to Match Cove Depth

Cove Width

Edge Distance

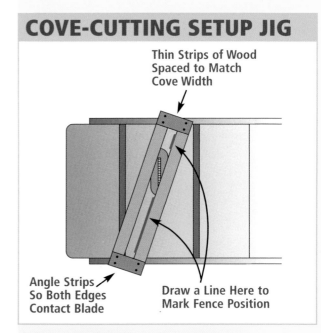

COVE-CUTTING SETUP JIG

Thin Strips of Wood Spaced to Match Cove Width

Angle Strips So Both Edges Contact Blade

Draw a Line Here to Mark Fence Position

Attach auxiliary fence

Now you can clamp an auxiliary fence (just a straight piece of scrap lumber) to the saw top so it's aligned with the mark you made (top photo). Since you'll be pushing the workpiece against this fence, make sure it's clamped firmly in place. Although not absolutely necessary, some woodworkers prefer to clamp a second fence parallel to the first so it's placed away from it the width of the workpiece. This creates a channel for the workpiece to slide in and keeps it tracking firmly against the angled fence.

First pass

Since you'll be presenting the workpiece to the blade in a manner the blade wasn't optimized for, you'll want to take many light passes (middle photo). It's best to take no more than 1/16" off in a single pass. Also, cove cutting creates a huge amount of dust, so make sure to hook up some dust collection. Because cutting coves removes a lot of wood, you'll want to use a slower feed rate than you'd use for normal ripping or crosscutting. Use a push block similar to the top push block shown in the middle photo on page 33.

Cleanup pass

As you near the finished cove depth, it's a good idea to make the last few passes even lighter, followed by a very light cleanup pass (bottom photo). This will help reduce scoring inside the cove, will clean up any torn fibers, and will produce the cleanest cove possible. Even with this technique you'll still need to smooth the inside of the cove. Try a custom sanding block: Attach a piece of self-stick sandpaper to the cove with the grit facing up. Then sand a foam block to the shape of the cove by rubbing it against the sandpaper. Finally, stick the sandpaper to the curved face of the foam block and smooth the cove with the foam block.

Resawing

Many woodworking projects call for thin stock — anything less than $3/4$" in thickness. You can buy thin stock, but it tends to be quite expensive. You can plane thicker wood down to the desired thickness, but this is hard on your planer — and a waste of good wood. A more cost-effective and less wasteful way to produce thin stock is to resaw a board on the table saw into thinner pieces. Resawing requires the workpiece to be cut on edge, so you must take safety precautions to prevent an accident.

Zero-clearance insert
The opening in the average saw throat plate ranges from $3/8$" to $5/8$". As a workpiece on edge passes over this opening, there's little or no surface to support the stock. When you finish cutting through the workpiece, there's a very real danger that the piece pressed up against the rip fence can fall down into this opening, possibly jamming up against the spinning saw blade. To prevent this and to provide maximum bearing surface for the workpiece, it's always a good idea to use a zero-clearance insert when resawing (top photo). See page 50 for directions on how to make a zero-clearance insert.

Auxiliary fence
Depending on the width of the workpiece you're resawing, you may or may not want to attach an auxiliary fence to your rip fence (middle photo). This isn't necessary for workpieces that are narrower than the maximum blade height of your saw. For wider pieces, it's best to use an auxiliary fence to help keep the on-edge workpiece from tilting as you cut.

Multiple passes
Whenever the workpiece you're resawing is wider than the maximum cut on your saw, you'll need to make the cut in two passes (see the drawing below). In most cases, it's best to resaw in two equal passes — that is, adjust the blade height to cut one-half the width of the workpiece.

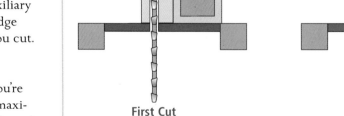

TWO-PASS SEQUENCE FOR RESAWING

First Cut

Second Cut

Featherboard

In addition to an auxiliary fence, smart woodworkers use a featherboard when resawing. This helps keep the workpiece pressed firmly against the rip fence as you cut, and also helps prevent the workpiece from tilting. Adjust the featherboard so it's aligned with the front of the blade as shown in the top photo. If you position it farther back on the blade, it'll cause the cut piece to press up against the blade and burn.

First pass

Once everything is set up, make a dry run by lowering the blade completely and pushing the workpiece over the throat plate. This will ensure that the featherboard is set correctly and will not cause the workpiece to bind. Then raise the blade to the desired cut, turn on the saw, and make your first pass (middle photo). Since you're removing a lot of wood, dust collection is a must. You'll want to use a steady, slow feed rate. The sound of the saw's motor will tell you if you're going too fast. If its pitch lowers, you're bogging it down and need to slow down the feed rate.

Second pass

With the first pass complete, flip the workpiece end for end, taking care to keep the same face pressed up against the rip fence, and make the second pass (bottom photo). There are two options here. One is to have the blade high enough to completely cut the piece in half. If you're using a zero-clearance insert, this works just fine. The only challenge is to guide the thin piece between the saw blade and rip fence safely past the blade. As long as you're using a tall auxiliary fence with the zero-clearance insert, this should be no problem. The other option is to lower the blade so you don't cut all the way through — just very close. Then you can separate the two pieces and hand-plane away the thin connecting piece.

Joinery:
Rabbets

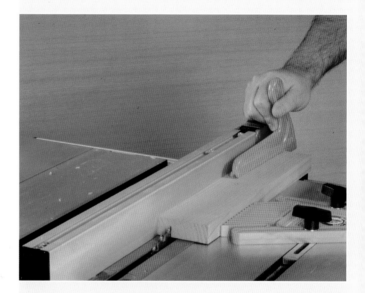

Along with the dado joint, the rabbet joint is one of the two most common joints used in woodworking, see the photo above right. Although a simple rabbet joint offers no mechanical strength, it does three important things: It increases the glue surface compared to a plain butt joint, it makes it easier to assemble projects as the inside shoulder creates a stop to hold parts in position, and it reduces the amount of end grain showing. There are a couple of variations of the rabbet joint that do offer mechanical strength (see the sidebar on page 72). There are two basic ways to cut a rabbet on the table saw: two passes using a single blade, and one pass using a dado set.

The two-pass method has both advantages and disadvantages. On the plus side, you don't need to change blades and it's relatively quick and easy to set up. The downside is that it takes longer to cut (only a problem if you're cutting a lot of rabbets), it's not as precise as cutting a rabbet with a dado set, and the inside corner won't be clean where the two passes meet compared to using a dado set.

Two-pass method: first pass
To cut a rabbet in two passes, first set the blade height and rip fence to make the desired cut. Make the first pass with the workpiece lying flat on the saw table, as shown in the middle photo. This will cut one shoulder of the rabbet.

Two-pass method: second pass
To complete the rabbet, reset the rip fence and blade height if necessary and make the second cut with the workpiece on edge, as shown in the bottom photo. It's important to make sure the waste piece will fall away from the blade as shown and not be caught between the blade and the rip fence. Otherwise, the waste will be pinched between the blade and the fence and kick back.

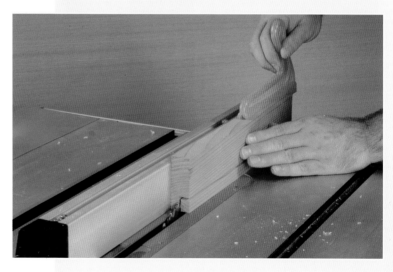

RABBETING WITH A DADO SET

Rabbeting with a dado set is a simple, precise operation. Since a rabbet is cut on the edge of the workpiece, usually with the workpiece lying flat on the saw table, the dado set would have to butt up against the rip fence. Not only is this unsafe, since there's a high risk of the dado set cutting into the rip fence and damaging both, but it's also a waste of time trying to get the dado set adjusted to the perfect rabbet width. A better solution is to use a dado set that's wider than the desired rabbet and bury a portion of the dado set in a wood auxiliary fence (see below).

Use an auxiliary fence. The simplest way to make an auxiliary fence for cutting rabbets is to clamp a scrap piece to the rip fence securely with screw clamps (top photo). Then lower the dado set completely and slide the fence partially over the dado set and lock it in place. Turn on the saw and slowly raise the spinning dado set into the auxiliary fence. Stop when the blade height is just a bit past the desired depth of cut, and then turn off the saw.

Set the blade height and fence. Now you can adjust the blade height using spacer blocks (as shown here in the middle photo) or with a rule or combination square for the desired rabbet height. Adjust the rip and auxiliary fences so the rabbet is the desired width (inset).

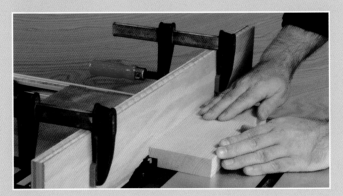

Cut the rabbet. Before you cut the rabbet in your finished stock, take a moment and make a test cut in a scrap piece. Measure the rabbet and adjust blade height or rip fence position as needed. Then cut your finished workpiece (bottom photo). Take care to use a push block as you finish the cut to keep your hand away from the spinning dado blade.

RABBET JOINT VARIATIONS

As mentioned on page 70, a simple rabbet joint offers no mechanical strength. Here are two variations of the rabbet joint that do provide some mechanical strength: the dado rabbet joint and the locking rabbet joint.

Dado rabbet joint. A dado rabbet joint is made by cutting a rabbet in the end of a workpiece and a dado in the face of the connecting piece (photo at right). The tongue that results from cutting the rabbet fits into the dado in the adjoining piece. You can cut either first, but it's generally easier to cut the rabbet (and resulting tongue) to fit the dado.

Cut the dado. The dado is cut easily in the face of the adjoining workpiece with a dado set by positioning the rip fence as a stop and using a miter gauge and backer block to push the workpiece past the blade (middle photo). Set the rip fence so the outer chipper of the dado set is away from the fence the thickness of the stock you're working with.

Cut the rabbet. All that's left is to cut the rabbet to create a tongue that will fit into the dado you just cut. Bury a dado set in an auxiliary fence and push the workpiece past the dado set with the miter gauge and a backer block (bottom photo). Check the fit and adjust as necessary.

Locking rabbet joint. A locking rabbet joint is cut much like the dado rabbet joint except that the tongue is formed differently. It's made by cutting a kerf on the edge of the workpiece and then trimming the tongue to length to fit the dado; see the drawing at left. The advantage of this joint is that the end grain of the adjoining piece is completely covered; this makes it particularly useful for drawer fronts, where you don't want end grain to show.

LOCKING RABBET JOINT

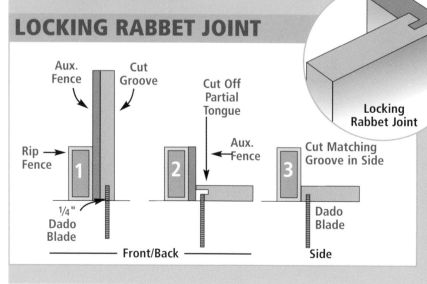

Locking Rabbet Joint

1 — Aux. Fence, Cut Groove, Rip Fence, 1/4" Dado Blade

2 — Cut Off Partial Tongue, Aux. Fence

3 — Cut Matching Groove in Side, Dado Blade

Front/Back — Side

Joinery: Grooves

Grooves are U-shaped channels cut with the grain; dadoes (page 74) are U-shaped channels cut across the grain. Grooves can be cut on the table saw with a single blade taking multiples passes, with a dado set taking multiple passes, or in a single pass.

Multiple passes: single blade

You can cut grooves with a single blade once the blade height is adjusted to the desired cut by simply moving the rip fence in increments matching the thickness of your blade (photo at right). In effect, you're cutting a series of kerfs until the desired groove width is achieved. Although simple, this technique is cumbersome if you've got a lot of grooves to cut. It also doesn't produce a groove bottom that is flat.

Multiple passes: dado set

For grooves wider than your dado set, you'll need to use the same fence-moving technique as described above (far left photo). The advantage here is that you'll have to move the fence fewer times, compared to cutting a wide groove with a single blade, plus the bottom of the groove will be relatively flat.

Single pass: dado set

When the groove you need to cut is less than the maximum cut of your dado set, all you need to do is select the chippers to create the desired groove width. Then set blade height and the rip fence and make the cut (near left photo).

CENTERED GROOVES

Many of the grooves you'll need to cut for your projects will be centered on the thickness of your stock. You can cut these by carefully measuring and making test cuts to center the groove perfectly. But there's a simpler, faster method. Use a blade or dado set that's slightly narrower that the desired width of cut. Then position the rip fence to roughly center the cut. Make a pass and then flip the workpiece end for end so the opposite face is against the rip fence, and make a second pass. This will make a perfectly centered groove. Adjust the rip fence as necessary to create the desired width.

CENTERING WITH TWO PASSES

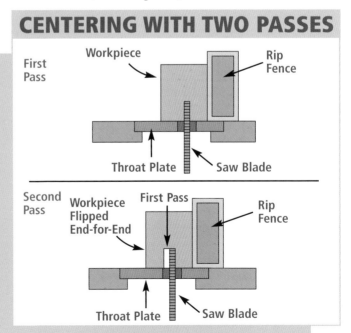

First Pass — Workpiece — Rip Fence — Throat Plate — Saw Blade

Second Pass — Workpiece Flipped End-for-End — First Pass — Rip Fence — Throat Plate — Saw Blade

Joinery: Dadoes

As with grooves (page 73), dadoes can be cut with a single blade or with a dado set. Unlike the groove (where chip-out and tear-out aren't a problem, since you're cutting with the grain), dadoes are cut cross-grain and both of these problems are common. Tear-out often occurs on the face of the workpiece and can be prevented with tricks similar to those used to keep plywood from splintering (see page 52). Using a backer board can prevent chip-out as the blade exits the wood (see page 75).

Single blade versus dado set

You can cut dadoes with a single blade with multiple passes, with a dado set in a single pass, and for wider dadoes with multiple passes, see the drawing below. Just like grooves, a single blade with multiple passes does not leave a smooth, flat bottom to the dado. You'll need a dado set to get that. Also, although you can use the rip fence to define one side of the dado, odds are you'll have to eyeball the other side. This can lead to dadoes that are too wide or too narrow. Your best bet for precision is to cut a dado with a dado set in a single pass.

Check the width

You can adjust the width of the dado by selecting chippers to be used with the dado set. The outside blades are typically $1/8$" thick. Inside chippers usually consist of four $1/8$" units and one $1/16$" unit. This lets you vary the width in $1/16$" increments. Unfortunately, you'll often need to cut an odd size, and that's where shims come in. Shims are inserted between the chippers to create slightly wider cuts. Some dado sets provide these; alternatively, you can make your own from plastic laminate or thin metal or plastic. One of the most reliable ways to check a dado set is to install it with the shims in place and measure from tooth to tooth on the outside blades with a dial caliper (left middle photo).

Remove the guard/splitter

Since a dado set doesn't cut all the way through the workpiece, you'll need to remove the saw guard and splitter assembly before making the cut (right middle photo). Lift out the throat plate and loosen any bolts as needed to lift off the guard and splitter assembly. Take care to retighten the bolts to prevent them from vibrating out during cutting.

DADO SET VS. A SINGLE BLADE

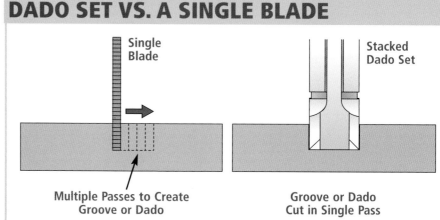

Single Blade

Stacked Dado Set

Multiple Passes to Create Groove or Dado

Groove or Dado Cut in Single Pass

Adjust the dado set height

Once your dado set is installed and the splitter/guard has been removed, set the dado set to the desired height. You can do this with a metal rule (as shown in the top photo), or with a combination square or a set of spacer blocks (see page 43).

Set the rip fence as a stop

All that's left is to position the rip fence as a stop to define the location of the dado on the workpiece (middle photo). Although many books and saw manuals counsel against using the rip fence in conjunction with the miter gauge, it's perfectly safe here. Since a dado is not a through cut, there's no chance of kickback occurring (as long as the rip fence is parallel to the miter gauge slot and the trunion is adjusted properly; see Chapter 6 for more on these adjustments). With longer workpieces, it may not be possible to use the rip fence; in this case you'll need to eyeball the cut. Make sure to clearly mark the dado location on the edge of the workpiece to make positioning it easier.

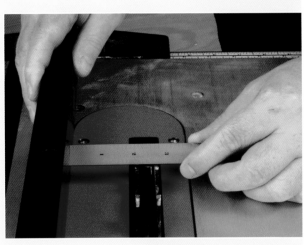

Make sure to use a backer board

With everything adjusted, go ahead and make a test cut on a scrap piece. Measure dado width, depth, and distance in from the edge to make sure all is in order; adjust as necessary. When you're ready to cut your project stock, make sure to slip a backer board between the miter gauge and the workpiece to prevent chip-out as the dado set exits the workpiece (bottom photo).

Joinery:
Spline Joint

Miter joints, where the ends of parts are joined together at an angle, are notoriously weak. That's because there's no strength in an end-grain-to-end-grain joint. One way to strengthen this weak joint is to cut grooves into the ends of the pieces and add a spline (top photo). This creates long-grain-to-long-grain glue surfaces, which are more than capable of holding the joint together over time. The trick is safely cutting the grooves in the ends of mitered pieces.

Groove setup

The safest way to cut grooves in the ends of a mitered piece is to use a tenoning jig or a modified tenoning jig (middle photo). For details of an easy-to-make tenoning jig, see page 81. The tenoning jig shown is fine for short pieces; but if you need to groove longer pieces, you'll want to modify the jig. Start by removing the vertical stop bar. Then miter one end of a strip and attach it to the face of the jig so it's angled at precisely 45 degrees. Now you can rest any length of workpiece on the angled strip to cut a groove in its end.

Cutting the grooves

To cut grooves in the end of a workpiece, adjust the rip fence to center the kerf on the end of the workpiece and adjust the blade to the desired height. Then simply push the jig holding the workpiece past the blade to cut the groove. A featherboard will help press the workpiece firmly against the jig as you make the cut (bottom photo). When all the grooves have been cut, cut a spline from hardboard as shown in the top photo, or from hardwood. If you do decide to use hardwood, you'll need to cut the spline so the grain of the spline is perpendicular to the grooves. If the grain runs parallel, the spline will split when any pressure is applied to the joint.

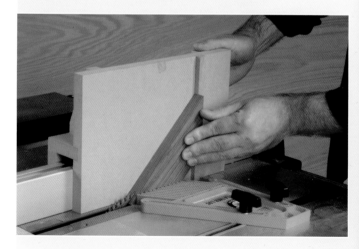

Joinery:
Lap Joints

A lap joint is formed when two parts are lapped over one another. In furniture construction, both ends of the pieces are typically notched so the surfaces end up flush with one another — this joint is technically called a half-lap and does an excellent job of resisting lateral movement (top photo). Making a lap joint on a table saw is simple. Basically, all you're doing is cutting long rabbets on the ends of the parts to be joined. The only challenge is getting the two halves the correct thickness so the faces end up flush.

Set the fence as a stop

To cut a lap joint (a half-lap joint is shown here), start by positioning the fence for the desired length of each half-lap (middle photo). Then install a dado set and raise it to roughly the desired height. An easy way to do this is to lay out the half-lap on the workpiece and align the shoulder mark with the edge of the dado set. Then slide the fence over until it butts up against the end of the workpiece. Before you lock the fence in position, check with a try square to make sure that the miter gauge is perpendicular to the rip fence.

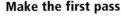

Make the first pass

Once the fence is in position, make a test cut. If what you're after is a true half-lap, where each cheek is the same thickness, there's a quick way to check for proper thickness. Make a first cut at the end of a piece of scrap the same thickness as your workpiece. Then flip the scrap over and cut the other face near the end. If the dado set is too low, you'll end up with a thin tenon. Continue raising the dado set slightly and repeating test cuts until the tenon just disappears. If the dado set is originally set too high, you'll get no tenon and you'll need to lower it. When it's perfect, make the first pass by butting the end of the workpiece against the rip fence, pushing it past the dado set with a miter gauge and backer board (bottom photo).

Remove the waste

Once you've made the first pass, pull the miter gauge back to its starting position. Slide the workpiece away from the rip fence roughly the width of your dado set, and make another pass. Continue cutting and sliding the workpiece over like this until you've removed all the waste to the end of the workpiece (top photo).

Cleanup pass

Even with an accurate dado set and careful cutting, the bottom of your half-lap joints will most likely be rough. There's a simple way to clean this up. Push the miter gauge forward until the front edge of the workpiece is centered over the apex of the blade. Then slide the workpiece away and toward the rip fence. Gently slide the miter gauge forward while you continue to slide the workpiece back and forth. This sawing motion will clip off any high points on the bottom of the half-lap, creating a smooth finish. Compare the lower, smoother of the two half-laps in the middle photo to the half-lap that this technique was not used on.

With one half of the joint done, you can cut the other half-lap using the method described above. Once you've finished the two halves of the joint, take the time to verify that the fit is perfect. Perfect here means that the faces of the workpieces end up flush with each other. If necessary, readjust the dado set height or the rip fence and continue cutting.

LAP JOINT VARIATIONS

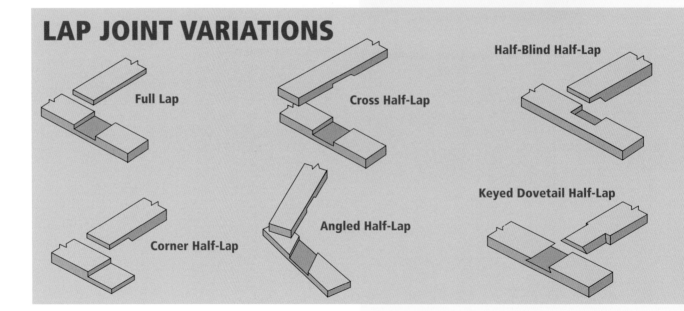

Full Lap

Cross Half-Lap

Half-Blind Half-Lap

Corner Half-Lap

Angled Half-Lap

Keyed Dovetail Half-Lap

Joinery:
Tenons

Without a doubt, the mortise-and-tenon is one of the strongest joints in furniture construction. That's why it's used almost exclusively for joining together high-stress or high-load parts, such as the sides of a chair or bench. The mortise-and-tenon has two parts: A hole (usually square) called a mortise is made in one part (see page 83 for easy-to-make mortises on the table saw), and a tenon is cut on the end of the mating part. Tenons are cut by removing wood on all four sides at the end of the part, creating shoulders (top photo). The tenon fits into the mortise and can be glued in place or held with dowels, fasteners, or even a wedge.

The best way to get a mortise-and-tenon to fit together is to cut the mortise first, then cut the tenon to fit. That's because it's much easier to resize a tenon than it is to recut a mortise. Tenons can be cut using a manufactured tenoning jig (as shown here), a shop-made tenoning jig (see page 81), or without any kind of jig, by making repeat cuts with a dado blade similar to cutting a half-lap joint (see pages 77–78). But instead of cutting just one face of the workpiece, you'll cut both faces and edges to create a tenon.

Tenoning jig: Adjust the blade height

To cut a tenon using a tenoning jig, start by setting the blade height to define the shoulders of the tenon. Since most tenons are long, you'll likely set blade height with a rule as shown in the middle photo or with a combination square (see page 43). Spacer blocks are generally too small for setting blade height.

Tenoning jig: Position the workpiece

Most manufactured tenoning jigs have some form of built-in stop and clamp to hold the workpiece in a perfectly vertical position. Before you mount the workpiece, first mark the tenon on one edge as an aid for positioning later. Then loosen the clamp and insert the workpiece, taking care to butt it fully up against the vertical stock. Check to make sure the end of the workpiece is resting perfectly flush on the saw top. Then tighten the clamp to secure the workpiece as shown in the bottom photo.

Tenoning jig: Adjust the stops

Most manufactured tenoning jigs have two sets of built-in stops; each defines one of the cheek cuts. Loosen the stop clamps and slide the workpiece in or out on its carriage to align the saw blade with the layout lines you marked on the tenon earlier. Once in place, lock each of the stop positions (top photo). Usually, there's an additional knob or lever that locks the sliding carriage in place once you slide it up against one of the stops to make a cut.

Tenoning jig: Make the cheek cuts

Replace your workpiece with a similarly sized scrap, turn on the saw, and make a set of test cuts. First cut one cheek (middle photo). Then loosen the carriage lock, and slide the carriage over for the second cheek cut. Tighten the carriage lock and make the cut (inset). Turn off the saw and remove the test piece; adjust as necessary, and when all looks good, cut your project stock. If your tenon has shoulders on all four sides, you'll need to reset the tenoning jig for these cuts — just make sure to make all cheek cuts on all your parts before doing so.

Tenoning jig: Make the shoulder cuts

To complete the tenon, you'll need to make the cuts that define the shoulders of the tenon. This is easily accomplished by first removing the tenoning jig and laying the workpiece with its face flat on the saw table. Clamp a stop block to the rip fence and adjust the fence so the stop block is the desired shoulder length. Then, with the workpiece up against the miter gauge, butt the end against the stop block, grip the piece firmly, and push it past the blade. This stop block technique prevents the waste scrap from being pinched between the blade and the rip fence, which usually results in kickback.

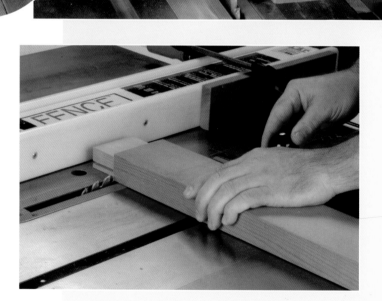

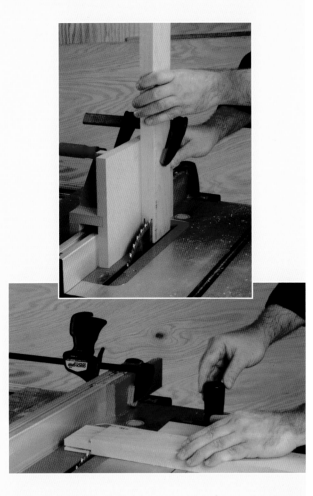

Fancy manufactured tenoning jigs like the one shown on pages 79–80 work great but can be expensive. You can make a simple tenoning jig for a few pennies that will work just fine; it just doesn't have a double stop system (see the sidebar below).

Shop-made jig: Make the cheek cuts

As with its more expensive cousin, the first thing to do when cutting a tenon with the shop-made tenoning jig is to set the blade height. Then slip the jig over your rip fence and position the fence to make the first cheek cut. Make a test cut on scrap, and if it looks good, cut your project stock (top photo). If the tenon is centered, all you have to do is rotate the workpiece so the opposite face is against the jig and make the second cut. If your tenon has four shoulders, reposition the fence and make the edge cuts.

Shop-made jig: Make the shoulder cuts

To complete the tenon, remove the jig and make the shoulder cuts. As when using a manufactured tenoning jig, lay the face of the workpiece flat on the saw table. Raise the blade so it just barely cuts off the waste. Use a stop block and position it and the fence to cut the desired tenon. Make the cut on a test piece first, then cut your project stock (middle photo).

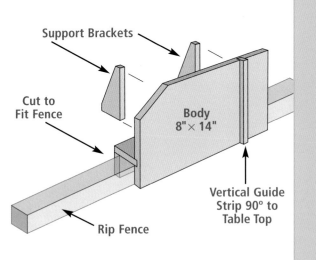

SHOP-MADE TENONING JIG

This simple shop-made tenoning jig is designed to slip over and slide on your rip fence. It consists of six parts: a body that accepts a vertical guide strip to present the workpiece to the saw at the proper angle, a two-piece fence clamp that attaches to the body, and two support brackets to keep the body perpendicular to the saw table, see the drawing at left. To make the tenoning jig, start by cutting the body to size. Then cut two grooves in the body: a horizontal groove to accept the two-piece clamp, and a vertical groove for the guide strip. Cut a guide strip to fit in the groove and glue it in place. Next, cut the parts of the two-piece clamp, glue and screw these pieces together, and attach this assembly to the body. Last, cut and attach the support brackets.

Support Brackets

Cut to Fit Fence

Body 8" × 14"

Rip Fence

Vertical Guide Strip 90° to Table Top

Double cuts with twin blades
For a production run where you need to cut a lot of tenons, another effective technique is to use two saw blades to cut both cheeks in a single pass, see the top drawing and photo. On most saws this method will work only with relatively narrow tenons, as the motor arbor will limit how far apart the blades can be positioned while still allowing the arbor nut to be installed and fully tightened. The secret to making this work is to use blades with matched diameters. Your best bet is to use the outside blades of a dado set as shown in the photo — they're already calibrated to be an exact match.

CUTTING A TENON IN A SINGLE PASS WITH TWIN BLADES

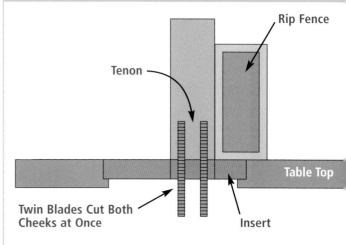

Rip Fence

Tenon

Table Top

Twin Blades Cut Both Cheeks at Once

Insert

CUTTING TENONS WITH A DADO SET

The final method for cutting tenons described here makes the cheek cuts with a dado set. The advantage is that no shoulder cuts are required — the dado set will remove all the waste when the cheek is cut. You can use this technique with any tenoning jig.

Cut one cheek. After you install the dado set, adjust the height for the desired tenon length and make a test cut on a scrap piece (photo at left). When satisfied, cut your project stock, taking care to slip a backer block between the jig and the workpiece — dado sets will create tremendous chip-out as they exit the workpiece if you don't back it up with a scrap piece. Use a slightly slower feed rate than you'd normally use, as you're removing a lot of material here.

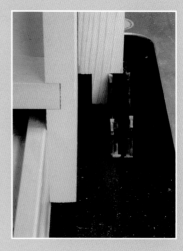

Flip to cut the other cheek. All you have to do to cut the other cheek (as long as the tenon is centered and not offset) is flip the workpiece over and make the cut. Here again, make sure to use a backer board and a slower feed rate. If the tenon is off-center, adjust the rip fence and jig for the second cheek cut, making sure that you've made the first cheek cut in all your project parts.

FAUX MORTISES

The other half of a mortise-and-tenon joint — the mortise — is not something you can cut normally on a table saw: The mortise is a hole or cavity cut into the edge or face of a workpiece. Mortises come in two basic types: stopped and through. A stopped mortise does not go all the way through the workpiece; a through mortise does. Both can be cut by hand or more commonly with a router and mortising jig.

There is, though, a nifty way to cut a through mortise on the table saw: Don't cut a mortise. Instead, cut a pair of matching wide dadoes on the inside faces of two pieces and glue these together to create a "faux" mortise. For this technique to work, the parts need to be of identical thickness, and care must be taken during glue-up.

Set up the cut. To make a faux mortise, start by installing a dado set, and then adjust the rip fence as a stop to define the shoulder of the wide dado (middle photo). Next, use a spacer block, rule, or combination square to set the height of the dado set to one-half the desired mortise width (inset).

Cut the dadoes. With the fence and dado set adjusted, make a test cut on a scrap piece. If all is well, cut your project stock by butting one end up against the rip fence and pushing the workpiece past the dado set with the miter gauge and a backer block. Make this first cut in all your mortise pieces. Then reset the rip fence to define the opposite shoulder and cut this on all pieces. Finally, slide the workpiece away from the rip fence as needed to remove any waste between the two shoulder cuts; repeat for all pieces.

Glue up the halves. Now you can glue up pairs of dadoed parts to form the faux mortises (bottom photo). One way to ensure that the halves align is to insert a scrap tenon "key" into the mortise during assembly. The only problem is that it's easy to end up gluing the key in place; to prevent this, apply a couple of coats of polyurethane to the "key" and let it dry before using it.

Joinery: Stub-Tenon-&-Groove

The stub-tenon-and-groove joint is one of those often-overlooked joints in woodworking — and that's too bad, because it's one of the simplest and quickest ways to make a sturdy frame-and-panel unit. Stub (or short) tenons are cut on the ends of the frame rails. These fit into shallow grooves cut the full length into the edges of the stiles; grooves are also cut full length in the edges of the rail parts. The full-length grooves accept the panel. The completed joint is shown in the top photo; the parts are exploded on the bottom photo on page 85 to show how they all fit together.

While short tenons, like those cut on the rail ends, won't make a very strong frame, that's okay: The strength of a stub-tenon-and-groove unit comes from gluing in the panel. Any woodworker who knows anything about wood movement might call foul at this. They'd say this is a bad idea since changes in humidity will cause the panel to expand and contract, causing the frame to eventually explode. They'd be right — if you used solid wood for the panel. The secret to stub-tenon-and-groove units is that the panel is plywood. And since plywood is dimensionally stable, that is, it moves very little with changes in humidity, you can safely glue it into the grooves in the frame. The resulting assembly is surprisingly strong — and stable.

As a general rule of thumb, the tenon should be approximately one-third the thickness of the stock. That means if you're using $3/4$"-thick stock (as shown here), you should make the tenons (and matching grooves) $1/4$" wide.

Cut the grooves in the stiles

To make a stub-tenon-and-groove unit, start by installing a dado set adjusted to the desired groove width. Then adjust the rip fence to position the groove in the stile pieces. Since the grooves in the stiles are typically centered, it's usually easier to take a double pass, flipping the workpiece end for end between passes to center the groove, as described on the bottom of page 73. Make a test cut on a scrap piece to verify that the groove is correct, and then cut the grooves in all the stile pieces with this setup (middle photo).

Cut the grooves in the rails

Once you've cut grooves in all the stiles, use the same setup to cut identical grooves in all of the rail pieces (bottom photo).

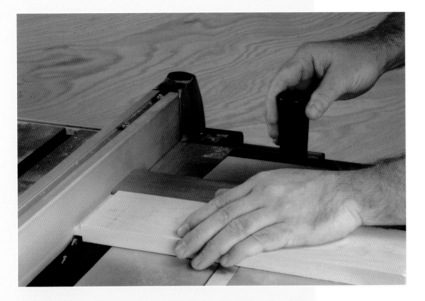

Cut the stub tenons on rail ends

With all the grooves cut, you can cut the stub tenons on the ends of the rails. Adjust the rip fence as a stop and adjust the dado set height, if necessary, to create a tenon that's a friction-fit in the grooves. Make test cuts on scrap pieces until the fit is perfect. Then use the miter gauge fitted with a backer block to push the rails past the dado set (top photo). Cut the tenons on all the rail pieces.

Rabbet the panel if necessary

Depending on the thickness of the plywood panel you're using, you may or may not need to rabbet the edge of the panel to allow it to fit into the grooves you cut in the frame pieces (middle photo). For example, 1/4"-thick plywood will fit right into the 1/4" grooves we cut in our frame parts. But the 1/2"-thick plywood we chose to use as the panel had to be rabbeted to fit. After cutting the panels to size, attach an auxiliary wood fence to the rip fence so you can bury the dado set in it. Adjust the dado set and rip fence as needed to produce a tongue on the edge of the plywood that will fit the grooves.

Glue up the unit

With all the joints cut and the panel cut to size (and rabbeted if necessary), you can assemble the frame-and-panel units (bottom photo). Take the time to dry-clamp each assembly without glue to make sure everything fits together nicely. With clamps on hand, apply glue to all the grooves and smooth it out with a glue brush (a plumber's flux brush works great here). Slip the panel in place and connect the stiles to the rails. Check all ends for flush and apply clamps. Wipe up any glue squeeze-out, and measure and compare diagonals to make sure the frame glues up square; adjust clamping pressure as needed to square the assembly.

Joinery:
Box Joints

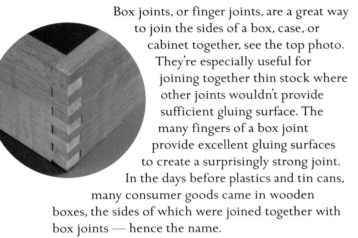

Box joints, or finger joints, are a great way to join the sides of a box, case, or cabinet together, see the top photo. They're especially useful for joining together thin stock where other joints wouldn't provide sufficient gluing surface. The many fingers of a box joint provide excellent gluing surfaces to create a surprisingly strong joint. In the days before plastics and tin cans, many consumer goods came in wooden boxes, the sides of which were joined together with box joints — hence the name.

Cutting box joints on a table saw requires a special box-joint jig to space or index the notches with precision. You can purchase one of these (see page 34), or make one yourself. See pages 110–115 for step-by-step directions for a shop-made box-joint jig.

Set up the blade
The first thing to do to cut box joints on the table saw is to install a dado set the desired width of the box joints in the saw and adjust its height. A simple way to do this is to use a piece of the stock as a guide. Just place a piece of stock face down on the saw top and slide it over against the dado set, as shown in the middle photo. Raise or lower the dado set so the end is flush with the face of the stock. Again, even though this is a relatively accurate way to set the dado set, you should still make a test cut to verify that it's correct.

Set up the joint spacing
The trickiest part of using a box-joint jig is setting it up to cut accurately spaced notches in the workpieces. All box-joint jigs for a table saw can only cut notches the size of the increment available in your dado set, typically $1/16"$ or $1/8"$ increments. This means you'll need to set the index pin of the box-joint jig away from the dado set the same distance as its

width. An easy way to do this is to use an equivalent size twist-drill bit. Just insert the shank of the bit (a $1/4"$ bit is shown here) between the index pin and the dado set as a spacer. Then lock the box-joint jig in place (for more on the shop-made jig shown here, see pages 110–115). Keep in mind that even though this is a fairly accurate way to adjust the jig, you may have to tweak the position of the index pin after you've made a set of test cuts.

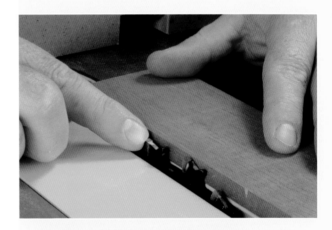

Cut the first piece

To cut the notches in the first workpiece, set the piece on end against the jig and slide it over until the edge butts up against the index pin. Then turn on the table saw and push the workpiece past the spinning dado set. There should be no problem with chip-out as the bit exits the workpiece because the jig will back up the cut. Remove the workpiece from the jig and slide it back to the starting position. Next, slip the notch you just cut over the index pin so the end is flat on the saw top, and make a second pass (top photo). Continue like this, lifting and moving the workpiece over until you've cut all the notches on the first workpiece.

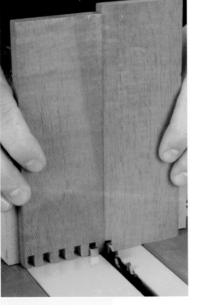

Cut the mating piece

The piece that mates with the first must have its notches shifted over so they can accept the pins cut in the first piece. To do this, use the first piece as a spacer to locate the first notch in the mating piece (middle photo). Make the first pass and then remove both pieces. Now slip the notch you cut in the mating piece over the index pin and continue cutting the notches as you did for the first piece.

Test the fit

When two adjoining sections are complete, check the fit of the parts. If they don't fit together, you'll need to increase the spacing between the index pin and the dado set; if too loose, decrease the spacing. The pins should also be flush or slightly proud of the adjoining piece. If necessary, adjust the dado set height and make another set of test cuts — just make sure to always use scrap that's the same thickness as your project stock.

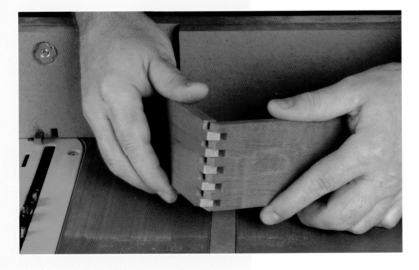

Using a Molding Head

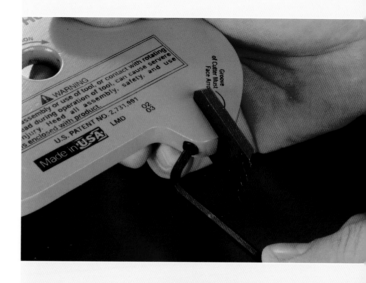

A molding head accessory basically turns your table saw into a shaper. By choosing and installing different cutters in the head, you can make simple or fancy moldings (top left photo), create precise glue joints, even clean up the edges of rough stock. Most molding heads come with a set of standard cutters, but many different profiles are available (see page 29 for more on this). They also come with a spacer that fits the molding head on the motor arbor to position the head so that it can be used with a standard dado throat plate.

Install the cutters

To use a molding head, start by selecting and installing the cutters. Follow the manufacturer's directions on inserting the cutters into the grooves in the molding head. Make sure to firmly tighten the setscrews that hold the cutters in place (top right photo). The last thing you want is one of these flying out at you when you turn on the saw.

Add a featherboard

In order for the molding head to cut precisely, it's important that you use a featherboard to keep the workpiece pressed firmly against the rip fence (middle photo). Lock the featherboard in place slightly back from the center of the molding head, as shown. This will apply pressure where it's needed — where the head contacts the wood.

Shape the wood

Adjust the rip fence as needed to position the cutter on the workpiece. Then turn on the saw (standing safely to one side), and make a test cut in a scrap piece. If the cut is true, shape your project parts (bottom photo).

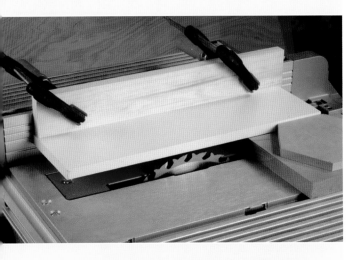

Pattern Sawing

Although many woodworkers think the only way to duplicate parts is to use a template and router fitted with a flush-trim or patternmaker's bit, you can actually duplicate parts on the table saw. The only requirement is that the parts being duplicated must have straight edges — curved parts cannot be reproduced. The secret to pattern sawing on the table saw is to add a special pattern-cutting fence to your rip fence.

Add the pattern-cutting fence

The pattern-cutting fence is nothing more than two pieces of scrap wood joined together to form an "L" (see the top photo). The only trick to using one is positioning it. What you're after here is to attach the pattern-cutting fence to your rip fence so that the horizontal piece is flush with the outer edge of the saw blade and just barely above the tips of the blade. The horizontal piece needs to be wider than the largest waste piece that you'll be trimming off the workpiece to be duplicated.

Attach the pattern to the workpiece

Cut your pattern to size (we're duplicating a hexagon-shaped base for a set of canisters). Attach the pattern to your workpiece with double-sided tape, taking care to position the pattern on the workpiece so the grain of the workpiece is oriented in the desired way (middle photo).

Make the pattern cuts

Now you can turn on the saw and duplicate the part. Simply butt one side of the pattern against the pattern-cutting fence and push the workpiece past the blade. Since the blade is aligned with the edge of the pattern-cutting fence, the workpiece is cut to match the pattern (bottom photo). Repeat for the remaining sides of the pattern. When you've cut one piece, turn off the saw and clean out the waste pieces between the blade and the rip fence to prevent them from kicking back.

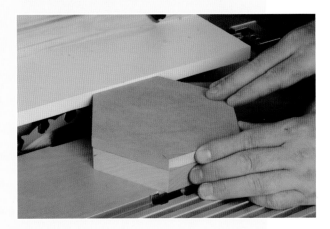

Making Raised Panels

Cabinet doors, sides of chests, and cases are often made using frame-and-panel construction. The frame consists of vertical stiles and horizontal rails, commonly joined with mortise-and-tenon or cope-and-stick joints. Grooves are cut along the inside edges to accept a panel that usually "floats" in the frame, letting it expand and contract as the seasons change. The panel is typically pinned to the rails in the center to keep it in position.

Panels can be plain flat pieces or have their edges molded in a variety of profiles (top photo). Profiling the edges does three things: It creates an attractive panel; it reduces the edge thickness so the panel can fit in the grooves of the frame; and it "raises" the center of the panel, creating a richer, more 3D-like effect. Panel raising is a simple operation on the table saw. There are two basic techniques for creating raised panels: the one-pass method and the two-pass method. Both methods require the addition of a tall auxiliary fence, discussed below.

Add a tall fence

Because panel raising requires you to cut the workpiece on its edge, it's imperative that you attach a tall auxiliary fence to your rip fence to provide stable support to the workpiece, see the bottom left photo. In most cases, the auxiliary fence is best attached to the rip fence from behind with screws. This way there's nothing to interfere with the workpiece as it's moved past the bit.

One-pass method

With the one-pass method, you cut the field (the angled part of the panel) and the shoulder (where the field meets the face of the panel) in a single pass, see the drawing below. This is simply a matter of tilting the blade to the desired angle and raising it to the desired height. There are two disadvantages to this method: The shoulder can only be as deep as the thickness of your saw blade (typically $1/8"$), and the shoulder will be angled, not perpendicular to the face of the panel. Once the fence and blade are adjusted, make a test cut on a scrap piece. If the field and shoulder are correct, cut your project panels, taking care to cut the end grain first, see the photo below. This way if there's any tear-out, it'll be removed when you cut the edge grain.

ONE-PASS METHOD

Tall Auxiliary Fence Screwed to Rip Fence to Support Workpiece

Rip Fence

Waste

Blade

Insert

TWO-PASS PANEL-RAISING METHOD

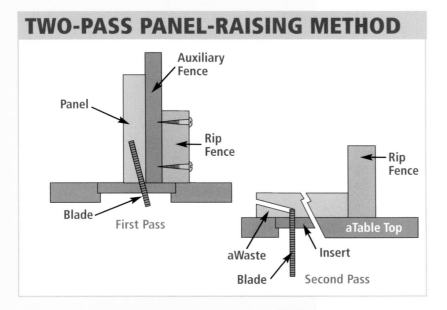

Auxiliary Fence

Panel

Rip Fence

Blade

First Pass

Rip Fence

aWaste

Insert

Blade

Second Pass

aTable Top

Two-pass method

The two-pass method creates the field and the shoulder separately in two different passes, see the drawing at left. Although this takes longer than the one-pass method, it offers a couple of advantages. First, you can cut the field anywhere along the edge of the workpiece. This means you can vary the thickness of the edges of the panel so they can fit into the grooves cut in the frame pieces that accept the panel. The depth of the shoulder can likewise be varied, depending on where you cut the field. If you want a $^1/4$"-deep field, you can make it so. Additionally, since you lay the workpiece flat on the saw top, the shoulder will be cut perpendicular to the face of the panel.

Two-pass met hod: Cut the field

The first pass cut defines the field of the panel. Adjust the rip fence and blade height to cut the desired field. Make a test cut on scrap wood and then cut your project panels once the setup is correct (middle photo). Here again, make the end-grain cuts first, then the long-grain cuts, to minimize tear-out.

Two-pass method: Cut the shoulder

Once the fields have been cut on your project parts, you can make the shoulder cuts. Adjust the blade back to 90 degrees and lower it so that it'll cut to the point where the field stops. Adjust the rip fence to serve as a stop and make a test cut on one of the panel scraps you cut earlier. If the shoulder is correct, make the shoulder cuts on all your project parts, taking care to make the end-grain cuts first to minimize tear-out (bottom photo). When you've completed your cuts, you may notice that the ends of the panel are a bit fuzzy. Remove any lifted fiber with fine sandpaper wrapped around a block. Make sure to sand with the grain to prevent cross-grain scratches.

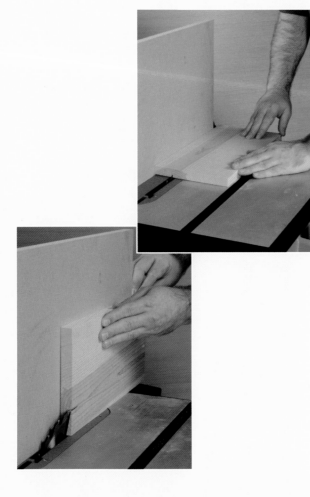

Kerf-Bending

There are three basic ways to bend wood: steam-bending, gluing up thin strips around a clamping form (often called bent lamination), and kerf-bending. By far the easiest of these three is kerf-bending (inset). The concept is simple: By making a series of relief cuts (kerfs) in the wood, the thin stock (often called a web) that remains is easily bendable. Kerf-bending requires a simple jig to space the kerfs precisely (see the opposite page), and some type of form to attach the curved piece to — an example of this is shown in the demilune table project on pages 160–164. The only mental challenge is determining the spacing of the kerfs to achieve the desired curve, see below.

Calculating kerf spacing

To determine kerf spacing, cut a kerf in a scrap of the project wood the same width as the finished piece. The depth of the kerf should leave between $1/16$" and $1/4$" of wood on the uncut side — a $1/8$" web works well for most woods. Then clamp the kerfed piece to a work surface with the kerf side up, as shown in the middle drawing at right. Now mark off the distance "R" equal to the desired radius. Raise the free end of the kerfed piece to just close the kerf, and measure the distance "S" shown in the drawing. This is the required kerf spacing.

The kerfing jig

The kerfing jig is simply a piece of scrap wood with an index pin attached to your miter gauge, see the top drawing. The most reliable way to make the index pin is to drive a woodscrew into the miter gauge about $1/2$" above the bottom of the scrap; then cut the head off the screw, and file the end smooth. You'll need to use a small screw for this, as the shank (pin) must be able to slide easily into a $1/8$"-wide kerf.

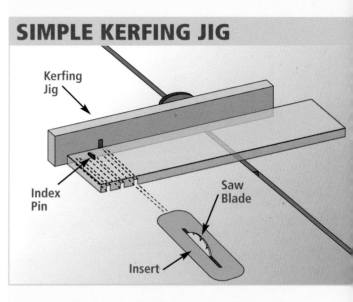

SIMPLE KERFING JIG

Kerfing Jig

Index Pin

Saw Blade

Insert

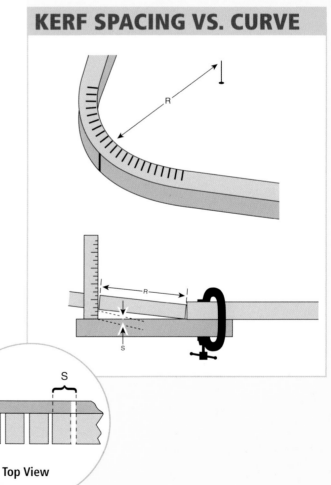

KERF SPACING VS. CURVE

R

R

S

S

Top View

Set up the kerfing jig

To set up the kerfing jig, place the jig against the miter gauge. Use a metal rule to position it so that the index pin is the correct distance "S" away from the blade (top photo). Once in place, secure the jig to the miter gauge with screws.

Cut the kerfs

Make a couple of test kerfs to ensure that the spacing is correct. Then use the miter gauge to push the project piece past the blade. Return the miter gauge to its starting position. Lift the workpiece and slip the kerf you just cut over the index pin (middle photo). Cut another kerf and repeat this process until all the kerfs are cut. Make sure to press the workpiece flat against the saw top as you make each cut, since the kerfed piece will tend to bow up slightly as it's kerfed. Pressing down keeps all the webs the same thickness and ensures a smooth bend.

Check the bend

When all the kerfs have been cut, check the curve to make sure it will bend around the desired radius (bottom photo). If you've got the bending form handy that the piece is kerfed to fit on, position the kerfed piece on the form and gently bend the piece around the curve. If necessary, adjust the spacing or cut the web slightly thinner to allow the piece to bend more.

Jointing on the Table Saw

The final advanced table saw technique we'll show here is unknown to many woodworkers. It allows you to joint wood with your table saw (inset photo). What's really nice is that you can joint wood as thick as the maximum blade height of your table saw. What's more, this technique lets you lay the workpiece flat on the saw table — not on edge as you must do with a jointer — so gravity works for you instead of against you. This makes it much easier to handle large pieces. All this requires is an easy-to-make jig, shown here.

Jointing jig

The jointing jig is just a short length of $^1/_8$" hardboard attached to a longer strip of plywood cut about an inch higher than your rip fence, see the drawing at right. This effectively creates an infeed and an outfeed table just like a jointer; the hardboard is the outfeed and the plywood is the infeed. Before you can use the jig, you'll need to create a curved recess for the blade in the hardboard. To do this, lower the saw blade completely and clamp the jointing jig to your rip fence so the end of the hardboard is positioned roughly over the apex of the saw blade. Slide the rip fence over so the outer edge of the blade is flush with the face of the hardboard. Lock the fence in place, turn on the saw, and raise the blade to its full height. This will create a curved recess in the hardboard for the saw blade, see the top photo on the opposite page.

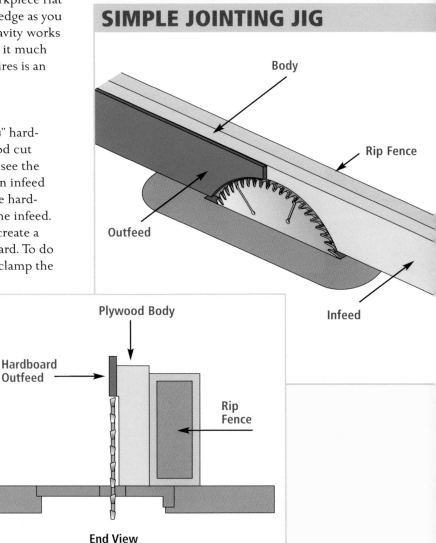

SIMPLE JOINTING JIG

Body

Rip Fence

Outfeed

Infeed

Plywood Body

Hardboard Outfeed

Rip Fence

End View

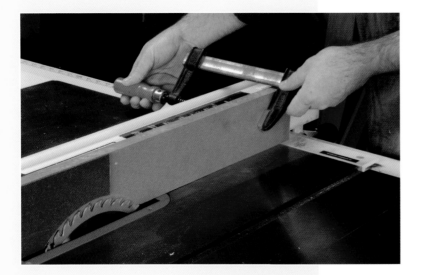

Attach the jig

When you're ready to joint some wood on the table saw, attach the jointing jig to your rip fence with clamps. Position it so the curved recess in the hardboard fits over the apex of the saw blade, see the top photo.

Adjust the jig

Now you can adjust the rip fence and jig to joint wood. What you're after here is to have the outer edges of the saw teeth align with the face of the hardboard (see the end view in the drawing on the opposite page). The easiest way to align these is to press a straightedge flat against the hardboard and slide the fence over until the straightedge just touches the teeth of the saw blade (middle photo). Once the teeth are aligned, lock the rip fence in place.

Joint your wood

When the blade and jointing jig are aligned, you can joint the edge of your workpiece; see the bottom photo. Turn on the saw and simply run the edge along the jointing jig. Make sure to transfer pressure to the outfeed side as the workpiece passes the saw blade, just as you would when using a jointer.

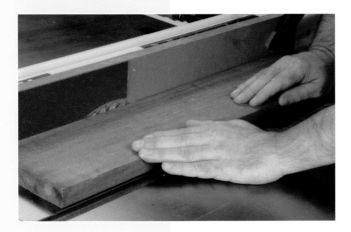

5 Shop-Made Table Saw Jigs & Fixtures

A table saw alone is a real multitasking woodworking machine. It can rip, crosscut, miter, and make a variety of joinery cuts such as grooves, dadoes, and rabbets. But when you add jigs to the equation, the capabilities of the table saw are almost endless. This chapter features seven jigs you can make for your table saw: everything from simple push sticks and featherboards to more complex projects such as a roller stand and a sliding cutoff table.

Each project includes exploded and detail drawings, materials lists, lots of photos, and complete step-by-step directions on how to build and use the jigs. Whether you build the miter gauge fence to add precision to your crosscuts or the box-joint jig to add box joints to your joinery repertoire, you'll find you can do more — and more accurately — with a table saw jig.

Once you start making and using some of the shop-made jigs shown in this chapter, you'll get hooked on the accuracy that jigs can add to your woodworking. Additionally, jigs make many operations safer to perform.

Push Stick

One of the most reliable ways to keep your hands safe while operating a table saw is to use a push stick to move the workpiece past the spinning blade. Push sticks come in wide variety of shapes and sizes. You can purchase them or make your own.

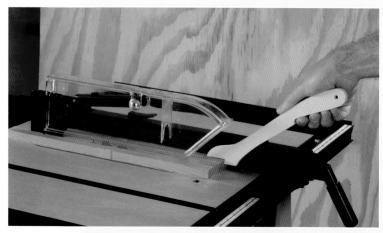

The push stick shown in the top photo is easy to make and readily replaced if it happens to hit the blade. It can be made from $1/2$"- or $3/4$"-thick scrap stock. Solid wood is fine, but plywood, with its cross-banded layers, will prove to be stronger over time. For a half-sized pattern for the push stick, see the opposite page. Note that there's a notch up high on the handle of the stick. This notch helps prevent your hand from sliding down if the workpiece catches on something.

Make a template
It's well worth the small effort to make a template of the push stick so that you'll be able to make copies as needed. The template shown in the middle photo is just a scrap of $1/8$" hardboard; plastic laminate works well, too.

Enlarge the half-sized pattern on the opposite page and transfer this to the template stock with carbon paper, or make a 200% copy and attach it with spray-on adhesive or rubber cement. Cut out the template and then use this to lay out the push stick on your plywood scrap. You can get two push sticks out of a single 3"-wide by 13"-long scrap.

Cut out the push sticks
Now you can cut out the push sticks with a coping saw, with a saber saw, or on the band saw as shown in the bottom photo. Take your time and keep to the waste side of the layout lines. Err on the side of making the stick thicker and not thinner, to keep it stout enough to push heavy stock.

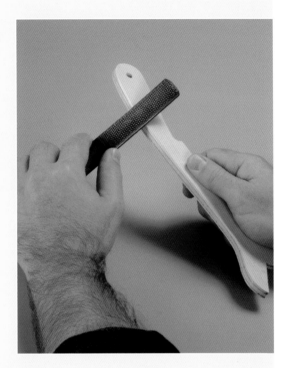

Consider making a set in three thicknesses, $1/4$", $1/2$", and $3/4$", so you can fit the stick between the rip fence and the saw blade/splitter guard assembly when ripping a variety of stock widths.

Final detailing

After you've cut the push sticks to shape, drill a $1/4$" hole near the top of each so that you can hang the stick on the wall near your saw, or so you can loop a string in the hole and hang the stick on your rip fence lock handle.

Then sand the edges smooth and, if desired, round over the edges of the handle with a file as shown in the top photo to make it comfortable to grip. Alternatively, run a $1/8$" roundover bit or a chamfer bit set for a $1/8$" cut around the handle ends to soften the edges. This takes only a minute or two, and by making the push stick more comfortable, you'll tend to reach for it more often.

PUSH STICK PATTERN

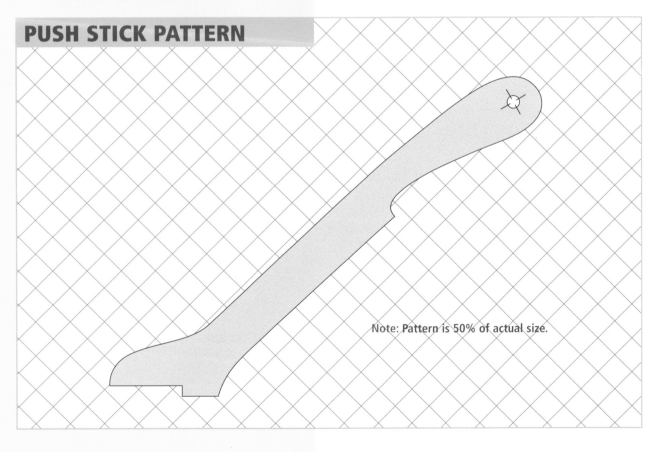

Note: Pattern is 50% of actual size.

Featherboard

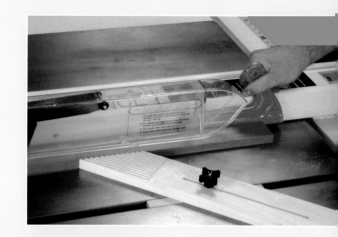

In addition to using a push stick (like the one shown on pages 98–99), using a featherboard is the second most reliable way to keep your hands away from a spinning blade. A featherboard has a set of flexible fingers at its end. When clamped against a workpiece, these fingers not only press the workpiece into the rip fence to ensure an accurate cut, but also help prevent kickback. That's because the fingers are angled and allow the workpiece to be fed in only one direction.

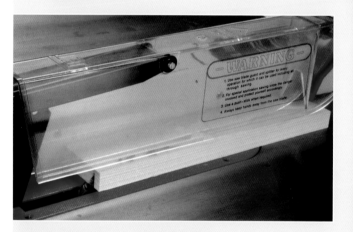

You can buy featherboards or make one yourself. The shop-made version shown in the top photo is designed to slide back and forth in the miter gauge slot, and it locks in place with a simple homemade clamp system. It's adjustable to handle a variety of stock widths and is both easy to make and easy to use.

Cut the runner to width
To make the featherboard, start by making the runner that slides in the miter gauge slot; see the materials list and the exploded view on the opposite page. The runner is cut to match the width and depth of your miter gauge slot. For most saws, this will be $1/2$" thick and $3/4$" wide; the runner is 8" long. The safest way to cut this is to rip a wide piece so the waste piece is $1/2$" wide, as shown in the middle photo.

Drill clamp holes in the runner
The homemade clamp consists of a $1/4$" × 2" machine bolt, a $1/4$" washer, and a $1/4$" plastic knob; see the cross section drawing on page 102. Here's how it works. The bolt fits in a countersunk hole centered on a short lengthwise slot cut in the runner. The bolt passes through the featherboard, and a plastic knob is threaded on the end. As the plastic knob is tightened, it pulls the bolt up, which in turn forces the runner to expand in the miter gauge slot to lock it in place.

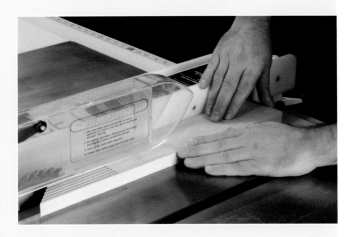

Drill a ¹/₄" hole centered on the width and length of the runner (bottom photo on page 100). Then countersink this so that a bolt inserted in the hole will be flush with the face of the runner. Next, cut a 2"-long kerf lengthwise in the runner centered on the hole. This can be done easily with a coping saw.

Cut the fingers in featherboard

Now you can work on the featherboard. Begin by cutting a blank to size and mitering the end at 45 degrees. Then cut the fingers. The simplest way to do this is to make a series of saw kerfs, moving the rip fence over in ¹/₈" increments as shown in the top photo. Make sure to draw a line across the featherboard to provide a visual reference so you'll know when to stop each kerf cut.

Alternatively, you can clamp a stop block to the rip fence to limit the kerf cuts. The safest way to make these cuts is to adjust the fence, turn on the saw, and push the blank forward until the blade meets the drawn line. Then turn off the saw, pull the blank back, and repeat for the next kerf. Continue like this until all the fingers are formed.

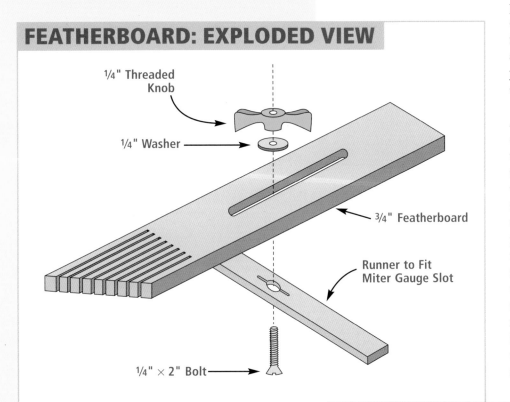

FEATHERBOARD: EXPLODED VIEW

¹/₄" Threaded Knob

¹/₄" Washer

³/₄" Featherboard

Runner to Fit Miter Gauge Slot

¹/₄" × 2" Bolt

MATERIALS LIST

Part	Quantity	Dimensions
Runner	1	³/₄" × 8" − ¹/₂"
Featherboard	1	3" × 18" − ³/₄"
Machine bolt	1	¹/₄" × 2"
Washer	1	¹/₄"
Plastic knob	1	¹/₄" threads

Cut the slot in the featherboard

In order for the featherboard to span across the saw top, a slot is cut to allow for adjustment. The slot is $1/4$" wide and 8" long. The simplest way to cut this is to start by laying out the ends of the slot, then drilling a $1/4$" start and stop hole at each end of the slot. This way, you can place one of the holes over a $1/4$" straight bit fitted in a router or router table, and slide the router table fence or edge guide on a portable router up against the featherboard. Then just turn on the router while keeping a firm grip on the featherboard, and rout away the waste in between the limit holes to form the slot as shown in the top photo. Alternatively, you can remove the waste by laying out the sides of the slot and cutting along these lines with a saber saw or coping saw to create the slot.

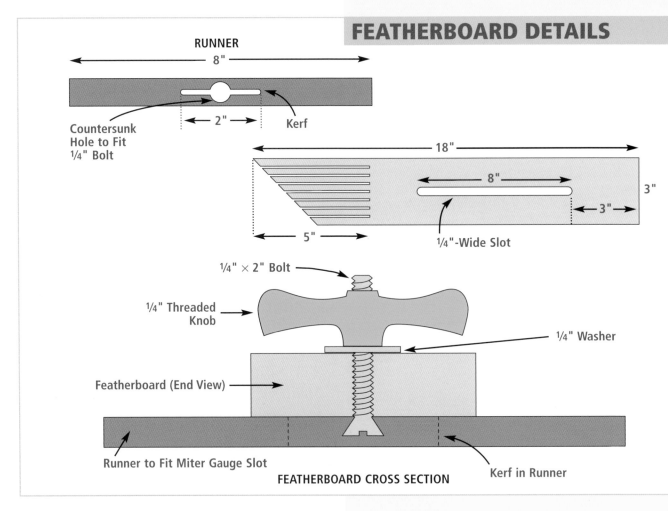

FEATHERBOARD DETAILS

RUNNER

8"

Countersunk Hole to Fit $1/4$" Bolt

2"

Kerf

18"

8"

3"

5"

$1/4$"-Wide Slot

3"

$1/4$" × 2" Bolt

$1/4$" Threaded Knob

$1/4$" Washer

Featherboard (End View)

Runner to Fit Miter Gauge Slot

Kerf in Runner

FEATHERBOARD CROSS SECTION

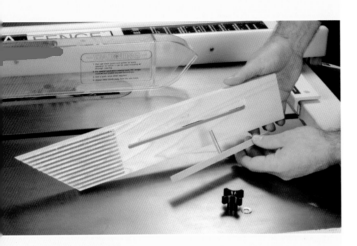

Assemble the featherboard

With all the parts complete, you can assemble the featherboard. Start by inserting the machine bolt through the hole in the runner. Then position the featherboard over the machine bolt. Slip on the $1/4$" washer and thread on the $1/4$" plastic knob to complete the assembly.

USING THE FEATHERBOARD

Position the featherboard. To use the featherboard, first adjust your rip fence for the desired cut. Then butt the workpiece you'll be cutting up against the rip fence. Next, place the featherboard in the appropriate miter gauge slot. Loosen the plastic knob and slide the angled end of the featherboard over until it butts up against the workpiece as shown in the bottom left photo.

Lock the featherboard in place. Now tighten the plastic knob just so it's friction-tight. Remove the workpiece and slide the featherboard over about another $1/8$", and fully tighten the plastic knob to lock the featherboard in place, as shown in the bottom right photo. Sliding the featherboard over like this will put tension on the fingers as the workpiece is pushed past it. This ensures an accurate cut and also keeps the workpiece from kicking back. **Warning:** The featherboard will not help prevent kickback if you do not put the fingers in tension against the workpiece. After you've locked the featherboard in place, it's a good idea to lower the blade and make a test run. You want to make sure the featherboard is positioned properly and the fingers are in tension, but not so much that you'll be prevented from pushing the workpiece past the blade.

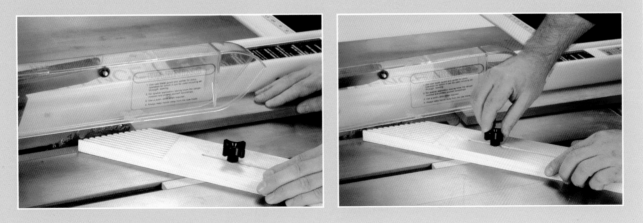

Roller Stand

Even table saws with large tops have trouble supporting long or heavy stock when you're ripping or crosscutting. That's where roller stands come in. Yes, you can buy metal versions of these, but quality units are expensive and typically have only one roller. The shop-made roller stand shown in the top photo offers better support with its four rollers, its height is adjustable, and you can build one for just a few dollars (assuming you have some scrap 2×4 lumber lying around). One of its biggest advantages over store-bought stands is that its base is very stable and adjustable. That is, there are levelers at the end of each foot that can be independently adjusted to compensate for uneven shops floors (and who doesn't have an uneven shop floor?).

Cut the half laps

To make the roller stand, start by cutting the upper and lower leg parts to size, see the exploded view and materials list on the opposite page. Half-lap joints are used to connect the upper legs with the roller supports and the lower legs to the feet. These are all $3^1/2$" wide and $3/4$" deep. Cut one half-lap on each end of the legs and centered on the length of the roller support and feet as shown in the middle photo. Fit your table saw with a dado set and cut the half-lap joints in all of the leg pieces as well as the feet and roller supports. Consult the exploded view frequently, as it's important which side of these pieces you cut the joint in.

Shape the feet and roller supports

Once you've cut the half-laps, you can shape the feet and roller supports. The ends of the feet and roller supports are chamfered as shown in the bottom photo. See the detail drawing on page 106 for miter size. The chamfers on the roller supports help prevent a workpiece from catching the ends of the supports as it slides onto the rollers. The chamfers on the feet are mainly for appearance but do tend to reduce the risk of tripping as you walk around the roller stand.

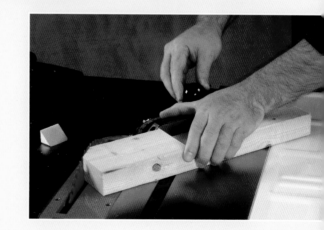

Cut grooves in legs

To allow you to adjust the height of the roller stand to match your saw top, the legs are made of two pieces held together with splines. The splines fit in ¼" grooves cut into the leg pieces. Set up your table saw with a dado set and position the rip fence ¾" away from the blade, see the cross section drawing on page 106. Make a pass on each leg, flip it end for end, and cut a matching groove on the opposite side. Do this for all four leg pieces.

EXPLODED VIEW

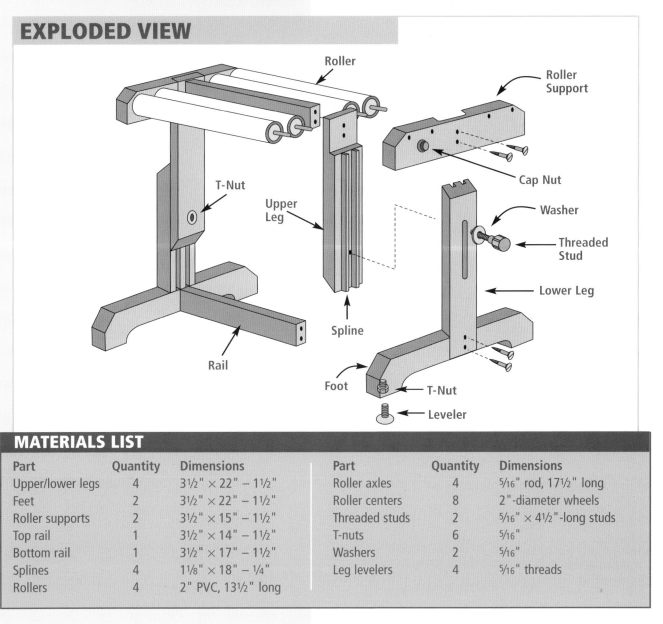

Roller

Roller Support

Cap Nut

T-Nut

Upper Leg

Washer

Threaded Stud

Lower Leg

Spline

Rail

Foot

T-Nut

Leveler

MATERIALS LIST

Part	Quantity	Dimensions	Part	Quantity	Dimensions
Upper/lower legs	4	3½" × 22" – 1½"	Roller axles	4	5⁄16" rod, 17½" long
Feet	2	3½" × 22" – 1½"	Roller centers	8	2"-diameter wheels
Roller supports	2	3½" × 15" – 1½"	Threaded studs	2	5⁄16" × 4½"-long studs
Top rail	1	3½" × 14" – 1½"	T-nuts	6	5⁄16"
Bottom rail	1	3½" × 17" – 1½"	Washers	2	5⁄16"
Splines	4	1⅛" × 18" – ¼"	Leg levelers	4	5⁄16" threads
Rollers	4	2" PVC, 13½" long			

Cut the slots in lower leg

Each upper and lower leg piece is held together with a threaded stud and a T-nut. Slots are cut in the lower leg piece to allow the piece to slide up and down over the threaded stud. Make the slots by drilling a pair of holes in each leg to define the start and stop points of each slot. Then fit a $^5/_{16}$" or $^1/_4$" straight bit in your portable router or router table, and clean out the waste between the holes as shown in the top photo. To guide the cut, use the router table fence on the router table or the edge guide on a portable router.

Drill holes for the roller axles

It's easier and more accurate to drill the holes in the roller supports before you assemble the leg parts. The best way to do this is to temporarily join the two roller supports with double-sided carpet tape. Then you can lay out the holes on one piece (see the detail drawing below) and drill the holes through both pieces at once as shown in the middle photo. This guarantees that the holes will be in perfect alignment for the roller axles.

OUTFEED ROLLER DETAILS

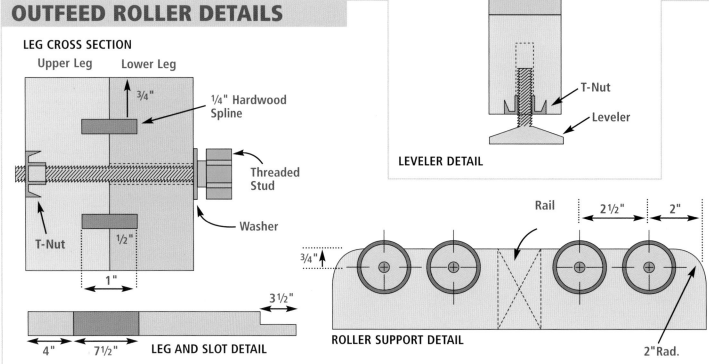

LEG CROSS SECTION

Upper Leg   Lower Leg

3/4"

1/4" Hardwood Spline

Threaded Stud

Washer

T-Nut

1/2"

1"

LEG AND SLOT DETAIL

4"   7 1/2"   3 1/2"

Foot Cross Section

T-Nut

Leveler

LEVELER DETAIL

Rail   2 1/2"   2"

3/4"

ROLLER SUPPORT DETAIL

2"Rad.

Drill the holes for the T-nuts

The last thing to do before you can assemble the leg units is to locate and drill holes for the T-nuts that hold the two units together. To do this, place each upper leg onto its mating lower leg, then insert a $^5/_{16}$" brad-point drill bit into the bottom of the slot in the lower leg. Tap the bit with a hammer to mark the hole location. Then drill the hole with the appropriate size drill as shown in the top photo. When both holes are drilled, tap in the T-nuts.

Assemble the leg units

After all the half-lap joints are cut, dry-assemble each of the units — the lower leg and foot, and the upper leg and roller support — to check the fit. If everything looks good, apply glue to the mating surfaces and assemble with clamps. Slip scraps of wood between the clamps and the workpiece to spread clamping pressure and protect the workpiece, as shown in the middle photo. When the assemblies are dry, cut splines to fit the grooves and glue them in place. You'll need only four strips — two for each upper leg piece. Once you've cut them to size, glue pairs of strips into the upper leg pieces. To make it easy for the lower leg pieces to slide up and down easily on the splines, sand a slight chamfer on the exposed edges of the splines once the glue dries.

Connect the lower legs

Now that the leg units are glued up, you can assemble them. Start with the lower legs. They're connected with the lower 17"-long rail. This is simply centered on the width of the feet and screwed in place as shown in the bottom photo. Use 3"-long drywall screws, and make sure the lower rail is perfectly plumb before securing. It's best to hold everything together with clamps, as shown, so you can easily adjust the rail position before screwing it in place.

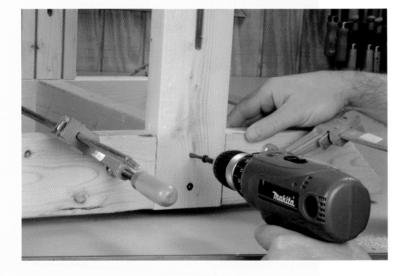

Attach rail to upper legs

Now you can repeat this operation for the upper leg units. Hold the upper leg units against the upper rail with clamps, and screw in through the leg units into the rail, as shown in the top photo. Make sure the rail is plumb before you drive in the screws. Any variation off plumb here will cause the stand to rack or twist out of square. If this happens, remove the screws, adjust the rail, and drive in another set of screws.

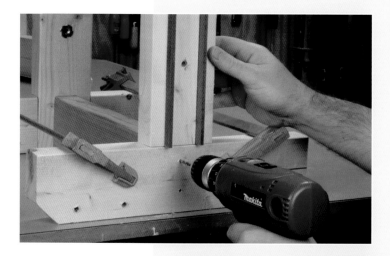

Connect the leg units

The upper and lower leg sections are connected with a threaded stud that fits into the T-nuts you installed earlier in the upper leg pieces. Align the splines of the upper legs with the grooves in the lower legs, and slide the units together. Then thread the threaded studs through the slots in the lower leg into the T-nuts in the upper leg. Make sure to slip washers onto the ends of the threaded studs before doing this. Tighten the threaded studs so that the upper leg is stationary, as shown in the middle photo.

Make the rollers

Cut the PVC to length and then glue a 2"-diameter toy wheel in each end, as shown in the bottom right photo. Note: You don't have to purchase wheels; if you own an adjustable hole-cutter, adjust it to cut a 2"-diameter wheel and cut out eight wheels. Yellow glue will work fine for securing the wheels, but epoxy works better. If you find that the wheels are loose, wrap a few turns of masking tape around the rim until the wheel is a snug fit (inset).

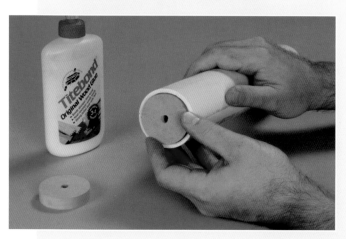

Attach the rollers

Now you can add the rollers. The rollers spin on lengths of $5/16$" metal rod and are held in place with metal push caps. Cut the rod to length and thread one at a time through a hole in one roller support, a roller, and the opposite hole in the other roller support, as shown in the top left photo. To add the metal push caps, butt a scrap block against one end of the axle, place a cap on the opposite end, and tap it in place with a hammer (inset). Move the block to the other end and tap on the remaining cap. Repeat for the other three rollers.

Add the leg levelers

All that's left to complete the roller stand is to add the leg levelers. Start by drilling a hole 2" in from the end of each foot to accept a T-nut. Then drive a T-nut into each hole so it ends up flush with the bottom of the foot. Then thread a leg leveler into each T-nut as shown in the middle photo. If the length of the shaft on the levelers permits, first thread a nut onto each before threading it into the T-nut. This way you can use the nut as a jam nut to lock the levelers in place once they've been adjusted. Alternatively, you can wrap a few turns of Teflon tape around the threads to help keep them from vibrating out of adjustment.

USING THE ROLLER STAND

To use the roller stand, position it behind or on the side of the stand and adjust it so it's level, using the leg levelers. Take care to position the rollers so they're parallel to the edge of the saw. If they're at an angle, they'll tend to pull or push the workpiece to one side as the cut is made. Next, loosen the threaded studs so they're friction-tight. Then raise the upper leg unit until the tops of the rollers are about $1/8$" below a scrap placed on the saw top, see the photo at right. Finally, fully tighten the threaded studs to lock the rollers in place.

Box- Joint Jig

Box joints are a classic way to join wood parts. They work particularly well with thin stock that's difficult to join since it doesn't offer much gluing surface. By cutting sets of matching notches in the ends of the parts to be joined, the gluing surface is dramatically increased. To cut box joints, you'll need a jig to accurately space the notches apart. The box-joint jig shown in the top photo attaches to your miter gauge and features an adjustable front that makes adjusting spacing a simple task. The adjustable front connects to a fixed front that houses a length of threaded rod (see the exploded view on the opposite page). A plastic knob that's threaded onto the rod is used to adjust the front (and index pin) back and forth. The adjustable front is then locked in place via a threaded stud that fits into a T-nut on the adjustable front.

There are a number of suitable materials to use as an index pin for your box-joint jig such as wood, UHMV plastic, and metal. If you decide to use a metal pin (as we did; it will hold up the best), you should know that metal bar stock is usually available only in $1/8"$ increments. You can find precut lengths in the hardware aisle in most hardware stores.

Cut a groove in the fixed front
Start work on the box-joint jig by cutting the parts to size, see the exploded view and materials list on the opposite page. Then fit a $1/4"$-wide dado set in the saw and cut a $1/4"$-wide, $1/2"$-deep groove along the full length of the fixed front, $3/4"$ up from its bottom edge, as shown in the middle photo. This groove accepts the threaded rod and filler strip added later.

Rout the slot in the back
The next step is to cut a slot in the back for the threaded stud that connects to the adjustable front. The simplest way to do this is to start by laying out and drilling a pair of $1/4"$ holes to define the ends of the slot. These holes are $3/4"$ down from the top edge and are centered 2" and 4" from the end of the back. This way, you can fit your table-mounted router

with a $1/4"$ straight bit and lower the back onto the bit without needing to make a plunge cut, as shown in the bottom photo. Position the fence $3/4"$ away from the center of the bit. Take three $1/4"$ passes to cut through the back, moving the workpiece from right to left each pass.

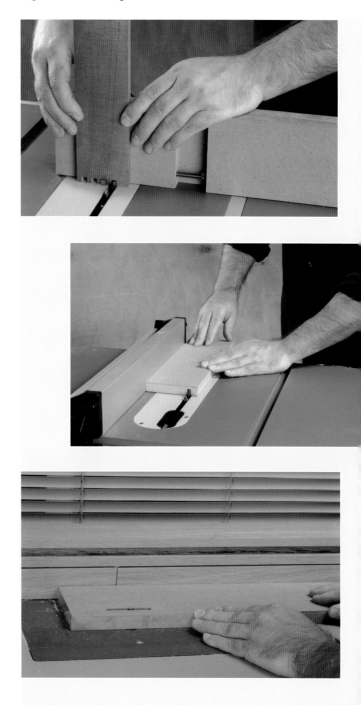

Glue the filler strip in the fixed front

Once the groove has been cut in the fixed front, you can cut a strip of $1/4$" hardboard to fit in the groove. The safest way to do this is to cut a wide piece of hardboard so the waste piece ends up the width you need to fit the groove.

Alternatively, you can cut this narrow strip with a sled as described on page 50. After you've cut the strip, glue it into the groove so it's flush with the face of the fixed front, as shown here in the top photo.

EXPLODED VIEW

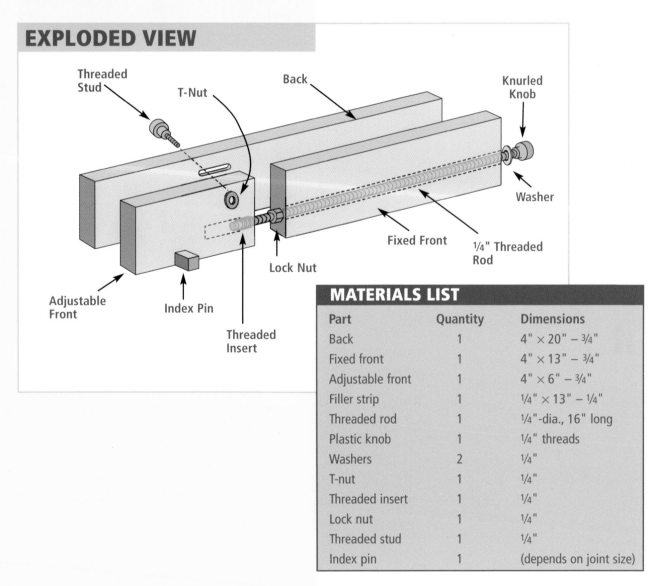

MATERIALS LIST

Part	Quantity	Dimensions
Back	1	$4" \times 20" - 3/4"$
Fixed front	1	$4" \times 13" - 3/4"$
Adjustable front	1	$4" \times 6" - 3/4"$
Filler strip	1	$1/4" \times 13" - 1/4"$
Threaded rod	1	$1/4"$-dia., 16" long
Plastic knob	1	$1/4"$ threads
Washers	2	$1/4"$
T-nut	1	$1/4"$
Threaded insert	1	$1/4"$
Lock nut	1	$1/4"$
Threaded stud	1	$1/4"$
Index pin	1	(depends on joint size)

Install threaded rod, lock nut, and knob

After the glue has dried on the filler strip, cut a piece of $1/4$" threaded rod to a length of 16". Thread this through the groove in the fixed front.

Thread a plastic nut onto the end of the fixed front as shown in the top photo, and thread a lock nut onto the other end. Continue threading on the lock nut until it snugs up against the end of the fixed front but still lets the rod spin freely.

BOX-JOINT JIG DETAIL

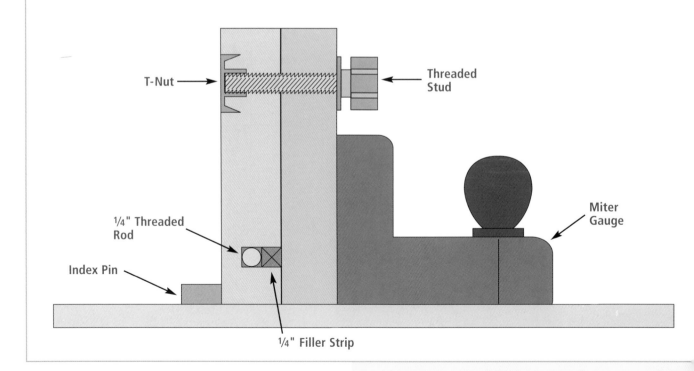

T-Nut

Threaded Stud

$1/4$" Threaded Rod

Index Pin

$1/4$" Filler Strip

Miter Gauge

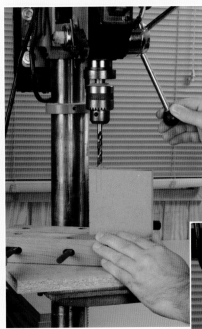

Drill rod hole in the adjustable front

The exposed end of the threaded rod in the fixed front threads into a threaded insert in the adjustable front. To allow the rod to slide in and out of the adjustable front, a clearance hole needs to be drilled in the end of the adjustable front. This hole is then enlarged in the next step to accept a threaded insert. To drill the clearance hole, clamp the adjustable front vertically as shown in the top photo. We used a wood handscrew for this, but you can also clamp the front to a scrap of 4×4 to hold it in place for drilling.

Drill a $5/16$" hole approximately 2" deep in the end of the adjustable front to match the location of the threaded rod in the fixed front.

Drill the hole for the threaded insert

Using the same clamping setup, you can drill an enlarged hole to accept the threaded insert. Switch to the bit recommended by the manufacturer of the threaded insert, and drill the hole as shown in the middle photo. Note: If you're using MDF, as we did here, you'll want to make this hole larger than the recommended size to prevent the MDF from splitting when the insert is driven into the hole. Drill a couple of test holes in a scrap of MDF first, and tap in an insert to test the fit. Keep enlarging the hole until the insert doesn't split the MDF.

Install the threaded insert

Now you can install the threaded insert. For the type shown in the bottom photo, all this entails is driving the insert into the hole with a hammer. Other inserts are threaded into the hole. The most reliable way to do this is to cut a 3" to 4" length of threaded rod to fit the insert. Then file two flats on one end and thread on a jam nut and the threaded insert. Snug the jam nut up against the threaded insert, and chuck the opposite end into your drill press. Lower the quill and turn the chuck by hand to drive the insert into the hole in the workpiece. When flush, loosen the jam nut and reverse the quill direction to remove the rod. Warning: Rotate the chuck by hand only.

Attach the adjustable front to the fixed front

The next step is to assemble the jig by gluing the
fixed front to the back. Apply a thin coat of glue to
the back of the fixed front and place it on the back.
Adjust its position so the top and bottom edges
and the ends are flush. Then clamp the two pieces
together. As shown in the top photo, spring clamps
exert more than enough pressure for this. Alternatively, you could screw the parts together or use a
caul and a set of bar clamps.

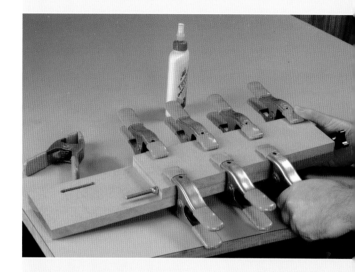

Locate the T-nut

The adjustable front is secured to the back by a
threaded knob that passes through the back and
threads into a T-nut installed in the adjustable front.
To locate this T-nut, hold the adjustable front onto
the back so the ends are flush. Then insert a $1/4$"-
diameter brad-point bit in the slot of the back, as
shown in the middle photo. Press the brad-point bit
into the front to make a dimple to locate the hole
for the T-nut. There are two holes that need to be
drilled for the T-nut. First, drill a $5/16$" hole through
the adjustable front plate to accept the body of the
T-nut. Then, drill a $1/16$"-deep counterbore on the
front face of the plate so
that when the T-nut is
installed, it won't pro-
trude and interfere
with the workpiece
(inset). Drill the $5/16$"
hole with a brad-point
bit, and the larger
counterbore (most likely
1") with a Forstner bit.

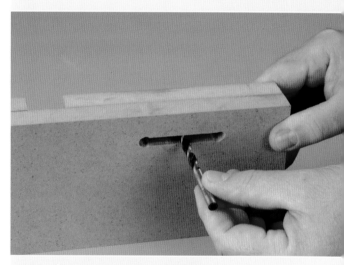

Install the T-nut

Now you can install the T-nut in the front face of the
adjustable front plate. Center it in the hole and
pound it in with a hammer until it sits below the
surface of the front plate, as shown in the bottom
photo. Alternatively, you could use a threaded insert
here, but the T-nut will provide the best grip without worry about pulling out if it's tightened too
much (which threaded inserts tend to do).

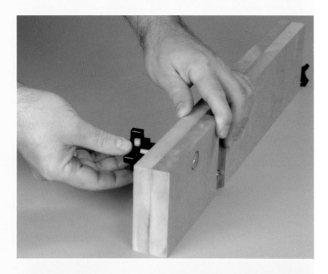

Assemble the jig

All that's left to complete the box-joint jig is to assemble the adjustable front to the fixed front and back. Do this by placing the adjustable front on the back so the threaded insert in the end of the adjustable front aligns with the threaded rod in the fixed front, as shown in the top photo. Turn the plastic knob on the end of the threaded rod to thread the rod into the insert in the adjustable front. Then thread the threaded stud through the slot in the back and into the T-nut in the adjustable front. Tighten this stud and attach the jig to your miter gauge, as described below.

Attach the jig to your miter gauge

Before you can use the box-joint jig, there are a couple of preliminary setup steps needed. Start by attaching the jig to your miter gauge as shown in the middle photo. To do this, first slip the miter gauge in the slot in the saw top. Position the jig on the miter gauge so that the adjustable front plate is centered on a dado set installed in the saw. Most miter gauges have a pair of holes in the back for securing auxiliary fences or jigs such as this.

Install the index pin

Now you can cut the notch to accept the index pin. The pin should match the size of the box joints you're planning to make, typically, $1/4$", $3/8$", or $1/2$". Set the dado set to match the thickness of the material you'll be cutting. For example, set it $1/4$" high as shown here to join $1/4$"-thick material. Then turn on the saw and slide the jig past the dado set, as shown in the bottom left photo. It will cut a perfect notch to accept your index pin.

Then turn off the saw and flip the box-joint jig upside down. Cut an index pin to length, and epoxy it into the notch you just cut (inset at right). Allow the epoxy to fully set and you're ready to cut box joints. For step-by-step directions on how to use this jig, see pages 86–87.

Miter Gauge Fence

One of the best ways to increase crosscutting accuracy on the table saw is to add an auxiliary fence to your miter gauge. An auxiliary fence can dramatically increase the bearing surface where the workpiece contacts the head of the miter gauge. With the average miter gauge head only running around 5" to 7" wide, this will help support the workpiece as it's pushed past the blade. And the more workpiece support, the more accurate the cut. Additionally, if the fence is lengthened so it extends past the saw blade, it will support the waste piece and help prevent tearout as the blade exits the workpiece.

The shop-made fence shown in the top photo does all this and more. It can be made of any length and attaches easily to your miter gauge. But what makes it even better is a slot on its face that accepts an adjustable stop block. With this stop block you can make repeat cuts all day long with super precision.

Cut the groove in the body
Begin work on the fence by cutting the body and face to a width of 4" and your desired length (the fence shown here is 20" long), see the exploded view and materials list on page 117. The stop block attaches to the fence by way of an ordinary closet flange bolt, commonly used to attach a toilet to the closet flange in a bathroom floor. The head of the flange slides back and forth in a T-shaped slot cut into the face of the fence, see the cross section drawing on page 118. To make this slot, start by cutting a $1/2$"-wide by $3/16$"-deep groove in the body, $1/2$" down from the top edge, as shown in the middle photo.

Glue on the hardboard face
The next step is to attach the hardboard face to the body. This is simply glued on and held in place with clamps until the glue dries, as shown in the bottom photo. In order for the recess to be cut in the front for the replaceable insert, do not apply glue in the 2" area shown in the detail drawing on page 117. Be sure to run a bead along the end of the body to attach the

end of the face to the end of the body — just keep glue away from the area indicated on the drawing. This way you'll be able to make the recess by taking two beveled cuts (see page 118 for more on this).

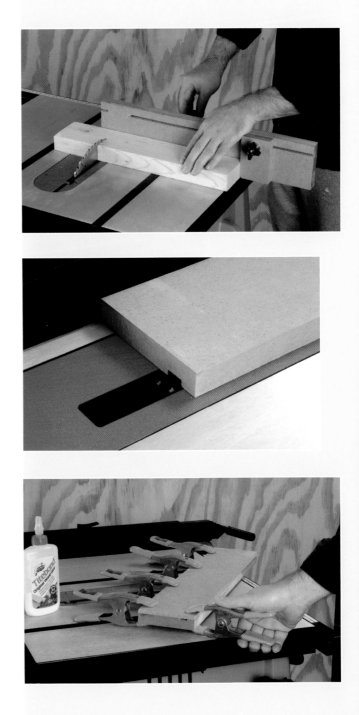

Cut a groove in the face

Once the glue is dry, you can cut the groove in the face for the shank of the closet flange bolt to pass through. This groove is $1/4$" wide and $5/8$" down from the top edge. Fit a $1/4$"-wide dado set in your saw and make the cut as shown in the top photo. Make sure to adjust the dado set to just cut through the hardboard. Otherwise you run the risk of cutting into the groove in the body, and this will cause the head of the closet flange to not slide smoothly as the stop block is moved.

EXPLODED VIEW

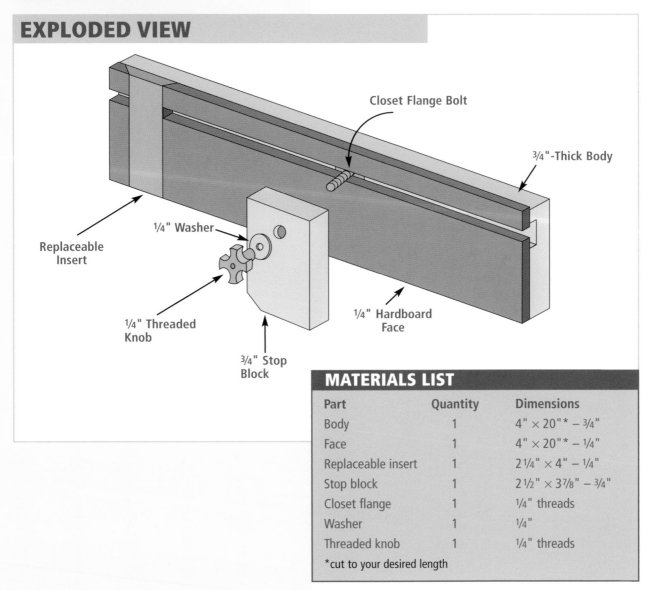

Closet Flange Bolt

$3/4$"-Thick Body

Replaceable Insert

$1/4$" Washer

$1/4$" Threaded Knob

$3/4$" Stop Block

$1/4$" Hardboard Face

MATERIALS LIST

Part	Quantity	Dimensions
Body	1	$4" \times 20"* - 3/4"$
Face	1	$4" \times 20"* - 1/4"$
Replaceable insert	1	$2 1/4" \times 4" - 1/4"$
Stop block	1	$2 1/2" \times 3 7/8" - 3/4"$
Closet flange	1	$1/4"$ threads
Washer	1	$1/4"$
Threaded knob	1	$1/4"$ threads
*cut to your desired length		

Cut the recess for the replaceable insert

With the groove cut in the face, all that's left to complete the fence is to cut the recess for the replaceable insert. Do this by tilting your saw blade for a 45-degree bevel and adjusting its height to a hair past $1/4$". Then mark the bevel cuts on the edge of the face and position the fence on your miter gauge to align one mark at a time with the saw blade. Turn on the saw and make the cut, as shown in the top photo. Move your miter gauge to the opposite slot to make the other cut. As you finish the cut, the hardboard covering the recess should be freed. Discard this piece.

Make the replaceable insert

Now you can cut some $1/4$" hardboard to make the replaceable insert. As this will get chewed up with use, consider making a half-dozen or so for the future. Tilt the blade to 45 degrees and bevel-rip the hardboard to width, as shown in the middle photo.

MITER GAUGE FENCE DETAILS

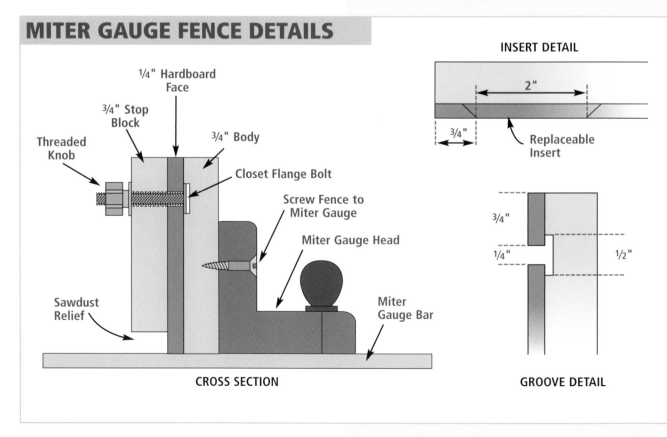

INSERT DETAIL

2"

$3/4$"

Replaceable Insert

$1/4$" Hardboard Face

$3/4$" Stop Block

$3/4$" Body

Threaded Knob

Closet Flange Bolt

Screw Fence to Miter Gauge

Miter Gauge Head

Sawdust Relief

Miter Gauge Bar

CROSS SECTION

GROOVE DETAIL

$3/4$"

$1/4$"

$1/2$"

Attach the fence to your miter gauge

To attach the fence to your miter gauge, position it on the face of the miter gauge so one end extends past the saw blade. Then secure the fence to the miter gauge by driving a pair of screws through the holes in the miter gauge and into the fence, as shown in the top photo. Take care to size the screws so that they won't poke through the front of the fence.

Add the stop block

Cut the stop block to size and drill a $1/4$"-hole centered on the block and $3/4$" down from the top edge. Cut a small miter on the inside corner of the block to serve as sawdust relief (see page 56 for more on this). Slide the head of the closet flange bolt into the T-shaped slot in the fence face, and slip the stop block over the shank of the bolt. Place a washer over the bolt shank and thread on a plastic threaded knob as shown in the middle photo (a wing nut will also work just fine here). In use, loosen the knob and slide the block over for the desired cut. Tighten the knob and double-check your measurement; readjust as needed. Also, to help prevent a workpiece from shifting or "creeping" during a cut, attach a couple of strips of self-adhesive sandpaper to the face of the fence near the bottom. The grit of the sandpaper will grip the workpiece and help hold it in place.

Installing the replaceable insert

The last step is to install a replaceable insert before using the fence. Just slide the beveled edges of the insert into the recess that you cut in the face, and push down, as shown in the bottom photo. This should be a snug fit, but not so tight as to bind. If necessary, trim the insert or cut new ones so that the fit is snug.

Sliding Cutoff Table

A sliding cutoff table at its most basic is a flat surface with runners that fit into the miter gauge slots in the saw top. By attaching a strip of wood to the rear of the table, you can butt a workpiece against it and push the table and workpiece past the saw blade to make a cut. The advantages to even this most basic table are many. First, if you attach the strip of wood so it's perfectly perpendicular to the saw blade, you'll end up with true 90-degree crosscuts. Second, the wide table serves as a carriage to easily cut wide panels or long boards, as the runners fit into both miter gauge slots to create a very stable base. Finally, the table itself serves almost like a zero-clearance insert (see pages 68–69) to support the wood fibers on the face of the workpiece, preventing chip-out.

The problem with most sliding cutoff tables is that they are dangerous. The reason? Most woodworkers will push the table by holding onto the wood strip and/or will press the workpiece against the sliding table to keep it from shifting during the cut. So when the blade exits the workpiece or the back of the strip, it can cut into the hands pushing the table or holding the workpiece. To prevent either of these, we designed an ultrasafe table that keeps your hands out of harm's way, see the top photo. This is done two ways. First, a built-in clamp presses the workpiece firmly against the sliding table so you won't have to do this with your hands. Second, a set of safety handles are mounted on top of the rear rail, and if used religiously, will prevent an accident as the blade exits the back or the rear rail. We even added a stop block system that allows you to make precise repeat cuts.

Cut grooves in the base

The base of the sliding table shown here is 24" × 36" and is cut from 3/4" MDF; this creates a flat, stable foundation. Center the base on the blade and mark the miter gauge slot locations on the edge of the base. Install a dado set in your saw, and cut 1/4"-deep grooves to accept runners cut to fit your miter gauge slots (middle photo).

Add the runners

Once the grooves are cut on the underside of the base, cut a pair of runners from a sturdy hardwood such as oak, or a high-grade plastic such as UHMW (ultra-high molecular weight), as described on page 61. Cut these to fit the slots and to thickness to fit into the grooves in the base. Attach the runners with glue as shown in the bottom photo, and let them dry overnight.

Cut the groove in the rear rail

Begin work on the rear rail by cutting it to size, see the exploded view and materials list below. An adjustable stop block attaches to the rear rail by way of a closet flange bolt (the type used to attach a toilet to the closet flange in a bathroom floor). The head of the flange slides back and forth in a T-shaped slot cut into the face of the rear rail, see the cross-section drawing on page 122. To make this slot, start by cutting a $1/2$"-wide by $3/16$"-deep groove in the face of the body, $1/2$" down from the top, as shown in the top photo.

EXPLODED VIEW

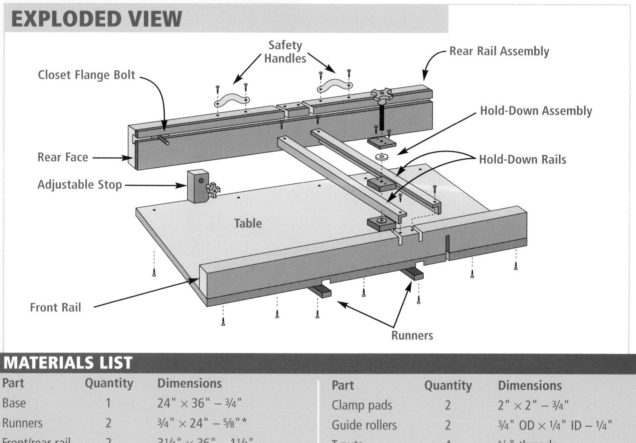

MATERIALS LIST

Part	Quantity	Dimensions	Part	Quantity	Dimensions
Base	1	24" × 36" – 3/4"	Clamp pads	2	2" × 2" – 3/4"
Runners	2	3/4" × 24" – 5/8"*	Guide rollers	2	3/4" OD × 1/4" ID – 1/4"
Front/rear rail	2	3½" × 36" – 1½"	T-nuts	4	1/4" threads
Rear face	1	3½" × 36" – 1/4"	Closet flange bolt	1	1/4" threads
Hold-down rails	2	1" aluminum angle, 24" long	Threaded knobs	3	1/4" threads
Adjustable stop	1	2½" × 3⅞" – 3/4"	Jam nuts	4	1/4"
Guides	2	2½" × 3½" – 3/4"	Washers	3	1/4"
Guide tops	2	2" × 3½" – 1/4"	Safety handles	2	3" long

*cut to fit your miter gauge slots

Glue on the hardboard face

The next step is to attach the hardboard face to the rear rail. This is simply glued on and held in place with clamps until the glue dries, as shown in the top photo. Spring clamps will work fine here, or you can use a caul and bar clamps.

Cut a groove in the face

Once the glue is dry, you can cut the groove in the face for the shank of the bolt to pass through. This groove is 1/4" wide and 5/8" down from the top edge. Fit a 1/4"-wide dado set in your saw and make the cut as shown in the inset photo. Make sure to adjust the dado set to just cut through the hardboard. Otherwise you run the risk of cutting into the groove in the body, and this will cause the head of the closet flange to not slide smoothly as the stop block is moved.

SLIDING CUTOFF TABLE DETAILS

HOLD-DOWN CROSS SECTION

- Threaded Knob
- Guide Roller
- Guide Top
- Aluminum Angle Hold-Down Rails
- T-Nut
- Guide
- T-Nut
- Clamp Bolt
- Clamp Pad
- Workpiece
- Table

HOLD-DOWN TOP VIEW

- Clamp Bolt
- Hold-Down Rail
- Screw Secures Top to Guide
- Guide Top
- Guide Roller

REAR RAIL AND STOP CROSS SECTION

- Rear Rail
- Rear Face
- Washer
- Closet Flange Bolt
- Threaded Knob
- Adjustable Stop
- Table

Cut notches in both rails

Once the rear rail is complete, you can cut the notches in both the front and rear rails that accept the aluminum angle guide rails. The notches are $7/8$"-deep, $1/8$"-wide kerfs cut 17" and $19\,5/8$" in from the end of the rails; see the exploded view on page 121 and the hold-down cross section on page 122. The hold-down rails are used in conjunction with the adjustable clamps. Since it's important that these notches align, temporarily fasten the two rails together with double-sided tape and cut the notches in both pieces at once, as shown in the top photo.

Install the rails

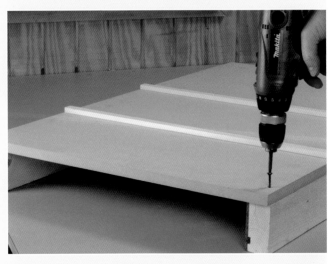

With the notches cut in the rails, you can separate the pieces and attach the rails to the base. Make sure to attach both flush with the same side of the base. The front rail can simply be screwed in place parallel to the front edge of the base. The rear rail needs to be installed perfectly perpendicular to the saw blade. To do this, attach one end with a screw and place the sliding table on the saw top with the runners engaged in the slot. Raise the blade about 2" and push the base forward until it cuts about halfway through the width of the base. Turn off the saw and butt the long blade of a framing square up against the rear rail. Slide it over until the short blade butts up against the saw blade. Pivot the rear rail as needed to make the short blade perfectly flush with the saw blade. Mark a line on the base, remove the sliding table, and clamp the unattached end of the rear rail to the base so it aligns with the line you drew on the base. Then drive in screws through the base and into the rail, taking care to keep screws out of the path of the blade.

Attach the hold-down rails

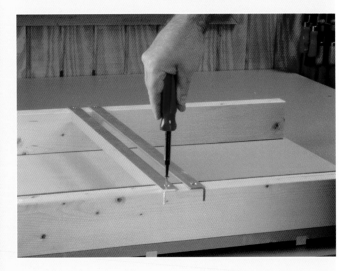

Cut the hold-down rails to length and file the ends smooth. Then lay out and drill a hole in the top of each piece for the screws that attach the hold-down rails to the front and rear rail. These holes are centered on the aluminum angle and are $3/4$" in from the ends. Countersink the holes and then insert the hold-down rails in the notches you just cut in the front and rear rails. Secure the hold-down rails with #6 × $1\,1/2$" woodscrews, as shown in the bottom photo.

Install T-nuts on the guides

Now you can turn your attention to the built-in clamps. Cut the parts to size per the materials list, and drill holes in the guides for the T-nuts that accept the threaded stud (see the hold-down top view and cross-section drawings on page 122). Drill these to fit the T-nuts, and make sure to counterbore the holes so the T-nuts will sit flush with the face of the guide. Then hammer a T-nut into each guide, as shown in the top photo. Finally, drill a $^3/_4$"-diameter, $^1/_8$"-deep counterbore in the opposite face of each guide to accept the guide rollers.

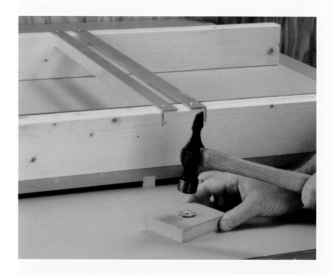

Attach the clamps

With the T-nuts in place, you can assemble the clamps onto the hold-down rails. Start by slipping a guide between the hold-down rails as shown in the middle photo. Then, with a guide roller in place, attach the guide top with a pair of #6 × 1" wood-screws; see the hold-down top view drawing on page 122. Test the action by sliding the guide back and forth on the hold-down rails; it should slide smoothly. If it binds, loosen the screws holding the guide top in place just a bit and test again. When it slides smoothly, thread the threaded stud through the guide. Once it passes through the guide, thread on a jam nut and thread the end into the T-nut on the clamp pad. Lock the pad in place by tightening the jam nut, as shown in the inset.

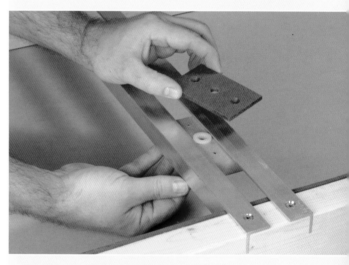

Add stop block to the rear rail

Cut the stop block to size and drill a $^1/_4$" hole centered on the block and $^3/_4$" down from the top edge. Cut a small miter on the inside corner of the block to serve as sawdust relief; see page 56 for more on this. Slide the head of the closet flange bolt into the T-shaped slot in the fence face, and slip the stop block over the shank of the bolt. Place a washer over the bolt shank and thread on a plastic threaded knob as shown in the bottom photo (a wing nut will also work just fine here). In use, loosen the knob and slide the block over for the desired cut. Tighten the knob and double-check your measurement; readjust as needed.

Add safety handles to the rear rail

To complete the sliding table, attach the safety handles to the top of the rear rail as shown in the top photo. Position these a comfortable distance apart and secure them with screws. When you're done, set the sliding table on the saw and raise the blade about 1" above the table. Turn on the saw and, gripping both handles, push the table forward to cut completely through the base. Turn off the saw, flip the table over, and drive a few more screws through the base and into the front and rear rail about 1" in from the saw cut. This will ensure that the base stays flat against the rails.

USING THE SLIDING TABLE

Using the hold-downs. With the power off on the saw, start by placing the sliding table on the saw top so the runners engage in the miter gauge slots. Adjust the saw blade for the desired cut and slip the workpiece onto the table so it butts up against the rear rail and is positioned for the desired cut. Then slide the built-in clamps so they're positioned roughly one-third in from each side of the workpiece. Spin the knobs on the guides to lower the clamp pads onto the workpiece, as shown in the top right photo. Tighten so the pads hold the workpiece firmly in place. Tip: Consider attaching a layer of self-stick sandpaper under the pads to help them bite into and hold the workpiece.

Making a cut. Now all you have to do to make the cut is turn on the saw, grip the sliding table by the safety handles, and push it forward to make the cut, as shown in the bottom right photo. When the cut is complete, turn off the saw, loosen the built-in clamps, and remove your workpiece.

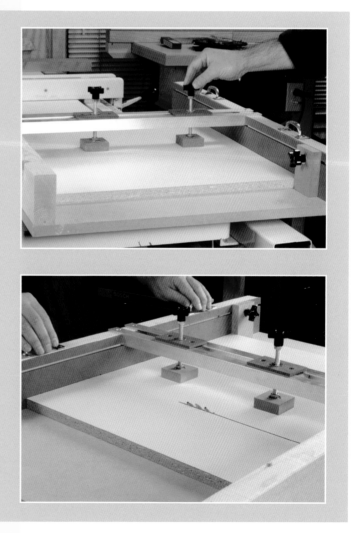

Taper Jig

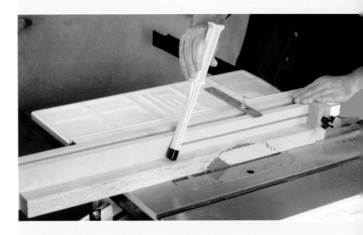

A taper jig for the table saw lets you cut tapers on parts such as table legs, bench legs, or stool legs (for a project that uses tapered legs, see the demilune table shown on pages 160–164). A good taper jig should also allow you to taper just about any part for any purpose. To be useful, a taper jig should be easily adjustable to cut a wide range of taper angles; it should also be adjustable to handle a variety of workpiece sizes. The shop-made taper jig shown in the top photo does both. Plus, it features a taper block with an index pin that holds one end of the part to be tapered securely in place as it passes by the saw blade.

Cut the slot in the adjustable rail

To build the taper jig, begin by cutting the parts to size, see the exploded view and materials list on the opposite page. Next, to allow the taper block to slide back and forth along the adjustable rail, cut a slot in the adjustable rail to allow the taper block's carriage bolt to pass through. An easy way to do this is to start by laying out and drilling a pair of $1/4$" holes to define the ends of the slot. These holes are $1^{1}/4$" down from the top edge of the rail and 1" and 17" in from the end of the rail. These holes let you lower the rail onto a $1/4$" straight bit fitted in your table-mounted router without needing to make a plunge cut (middle photo). Take three $1/4$"-deep passes to cut through the rail, moving the workpiece from right to left each pass.

Make the adjustable taper block

The taper block that slides along the slot in the adjustable rail is just a block of wood with two holes in it. One hole allows the $1/4$" carriage bolt to pass through it; the other accepts the pivot pin. Both holes are $1/4$" in diameter, see the detail drawing on page 128 for locations. Drill both holes (bottom photo) and glue the index pin into the appropriate hole with epoxy (inset).

Cut the slot in the adjustment bar

The next step is to make the adjustment bar that connects the fixed rail to the adjustable rail; this lets you pivot the adjustable rail out to the desired angle and lock it in place. Use the same procedure to cut the slot in the adjustment bar that you used to cut the slot in the adjustable rail (see page 126). Only this time, center the slot on the width of the adjustment bar and rout the slot to length of $5\frac{1}{2}$" centered on the length of the bar. Hold the bar in a clamp for routing, as shown in the top photo.

EXPLODED VIEW

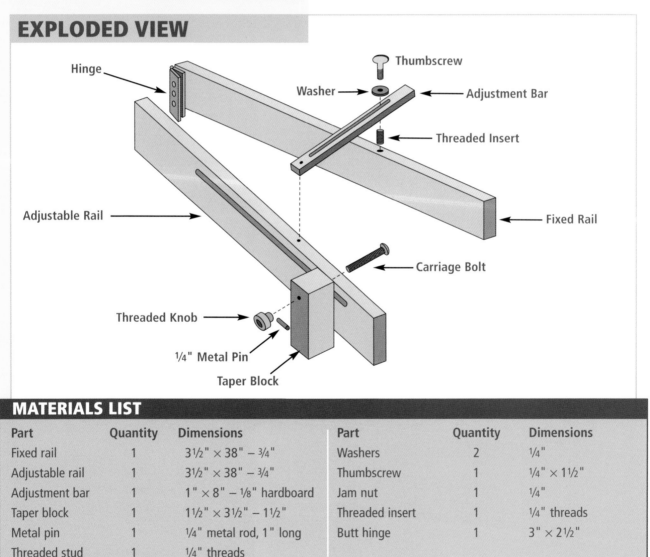

- Hinge
- Thumbscrew
- Washer
- Adjustment Bar
- Threaded Insert
- Adjustable Rail
- Fixed Rail
- Carriage Bolt
- Threaded Knob
- $\frac{1}{4}$" Metal Pin
- Taper Block

MATERIALS LIST

Part	Quantity	Dimensions	Part	Quantity	Dimensions
Fixed rail	1	$3\frac{1}{2}$" × 38" – $\frac{3}{4}$"	Washers	2	$\frac{1}{4}$"
Adjustable rail	1	$3\frac{1}{2}$" × 38" – $\frac{3}{4}$"	Thumbscrew	1	$\frac{1}{4}$" × $1\frac{1}{2}$"
Adjustment bar	1	1" × 8" – $\frac{1}{8}$" hardboard	Jam nut	1	$\frac{1}{4}$"
Taper block	1	$1\frac{1}{2}$" × $3\frac{1}{2}$" – $1\frac{1}{2}$"	Threaded insert	1	$\frac{1}{4}$" threads
Metal pin	1	$\frac{1}{4}$" metal rod, 1" long	Butt hinge	1	3" × $2\frac{1}{2}$"
Threaded stud	1	$\frac{1}{4}$" threads			

Install the threaded insert

Once the slot in the adjustment bar has been routed, you can install the threaded insert in the fixed rail. We used a $1/4$" threaded insert and installed it 8" in from the end of the fixed rail and centered on its width. If you use MDF as we did for the rails, you'll want to drill the hole for the insert larger than the manufacturer's recommendation. That's because the MDF will split easily when the insert is driven or threaded in. After you've drilled the appropriate-sized hole, drive the insert into the hole with a hammer, as shown in the top photo.

Connect the rails with a hinge

Now you can connect the adjustable rail to the fixed rail with a 3" butt hinge. The easiest way to do this and ensure alignment is to butt the ends of the rails together, as shown in the middle photo. Make sure the inside faces of the rails are facing up. Drill pilot holes in the mounting holes, and attach the hinge with the screws provided.

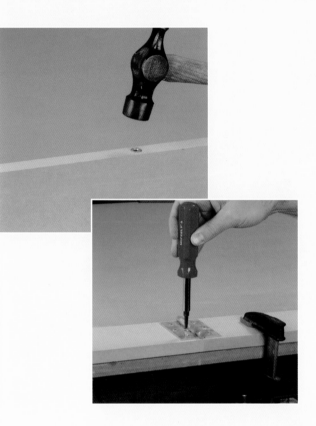

TAPER JIG DETAILS

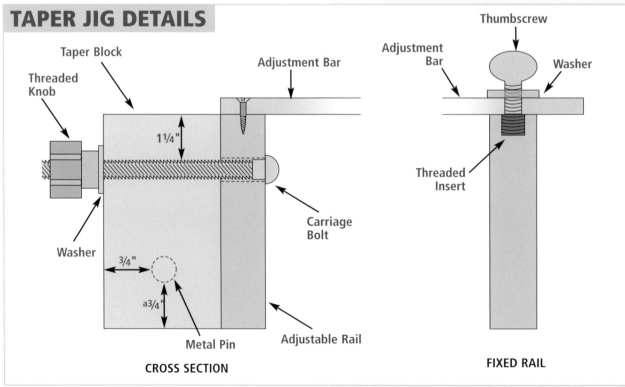

Threaded Knob

Taper Block

Adjustment Bar

1 1/4"

Carriage Bolt

Washer

3/4"

a3/4'

Metal Pin

Adjustable Rail

CROSS SECTION

Thumbscrew

Adjustment Bar

Washer

Threaded Insert

FIXED RAIL

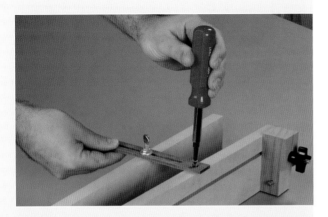

Attach the adjustment bar

To complete the jig, attach the adjustment bar that connects the adjustable rail to the fixed rail. Drill a countersunk pilot hole $3/8$" in from one end of the bar and attach this to the adjustable rail 8" in from the end. Make sure to drill a pilot hole before you drive in the screw, as shown in the top photo. Then thread a jam nut onto the thumbscrew and pass this through the slot in the adjustment bar and thread it into the threaded insert.

USING THE TAPER JIG

Clockwise from top left:

Drill an index hole in the blank. A hole is drilled into one end of the workpiece to fit over the metal pin in the adjustable taper block. Center this $1/4$"-diameter hole on the end and drill only $3/8$" deep. Then attach the workpiece to the taper block via the index pin.

Make the first pass. Adjust the jig for the desired angle by loosening the thumbscrew and pivoting the adjustable rail. Tighten the thumbscrew and adjust the pivot block position as needed to taper the desired length. Position the rip fence to make the cut, and push the taper jig and workpiece past the blade. Use a push stick to press the opposite end of the workpiece against the jig as you make the cut, as shown in the top photo on page 126.

Rotate to make the second pass. When the first taper is cut, turn off the saw, return the jig to its starting position, and rotate the workpiece to present the next leg face to the blade. Turn on the saw and cut as you did for the first pass. The index pin will hold the workpiece perfectly centered for the cut.

6 Maintenance & Troubleshooting

A quality table saw will stand up to a lot of use and abuse, and that's both good and bad. It's good because the saw will serve you well over time. It's bad because this will make it easy to put off or totally ignore maintenance. As with their other machines, some woodworkers won't do anything until there's a problem, such as inaccurate cuts, the motor bogging down, or even a major part failure.

This is a real shame, since most table saws represent a serious investment. And by the time a problem rears its head, something major — and expensive — could be wrong. That's why periodic maintenance is so important. The key word here is periodic. Keeping a saw cutting true requires an ongoing effort. The rip fence and miter gauge should be checked before a cut. The blades should be kept clean and sharp, and roughly once a year the trunion should be checked. In this chapter, you'll find step-by-step instructions on how to keep your saw cutting at peak performance.

All it takes to keep your table saw running in tip-top condition is some inexpensive supplies, a few basic tools, and the right know-how. Most maintenance procedures are easy and can be accomplished in an afternoon.

Table Saw Anatomy

Regardless of the type, all table saws have basically the same parts — what's different is the size and quality. At its simplest, a table saw consists of a blade attached to the shaft (or the arbor) of a motor, see the drawing below right. The blade protrudes through an opening in the saw top and is raised or lowered as needed. It can also be tilted from side to side for bevel cuts. The mechanism that holds the saw blade and allows it to be raised, lowered, and tilted is called the trunion (for more on the trunion and its parts, see pages 141–144).

The saw top on bench-top saws is typically cast aluminum; on contractor's and titling arbor saws it's cast iron. To increase the width of the top, cast or stamped metal extension wings are usually bolted to the sides of the cast top. Guide rails attach to the front and rear of the saw to accept the rip fence; slots in the saw top accept the miter gauge used for crosscuts. The opening in the saw top that the blade protrudes out of is larger than the blade so that you can loosen or tighten the arbor nut to change blades. To reduce this opening for use, a metal throat plate with a slot in it for the blade fits into a recess in the saw top at the opening.

At the back of the saw, a splitter guard assembly is attached either to the saw cabinet or to the trunion assembly. The splitter keeps the workpiece and the waste separate after the cut. The splitter also usually houses a pair of barbed anti-kickback pawls that prevent a workpiece from being hurled backwards in case it gets pinched between the saw blade and the rip fence. A blade guard attaches to the end of the splitter assembly and drops down to cover the blade — the clear plastic housing

provides a clear view of the cut, and it will pivot up and ride on the workpiece as a cut is made.

The saw motor is housed in the cabinet, and either attaches to the trunion or connects via a belt. Handwheels or knobs on the sides and/or front of the cabinet control the blade height and tilt; the on/off switch is usually located on the front of the saw within easy reach. Most saws have some sort of housing or cover to help direct dust out of the machine and into a vacuum or dust collection unit.

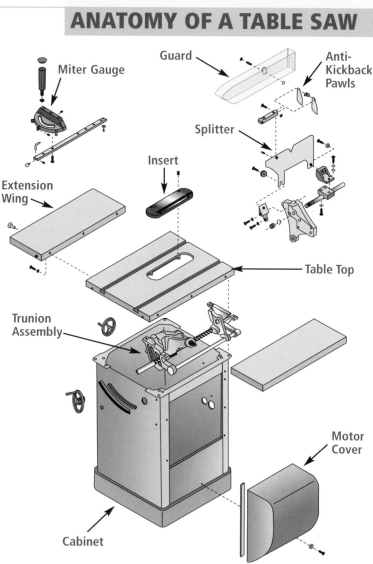

ANATOMY OF A TABLE SAW

Miter Gauge · Guard · Anti-Kickback Pawls · Splitter · Insert · Extension Wing · Table Top · Trunion Assembly · Motor Cover · Cabinet

Lubrication

One of the best ways to keep your table saw running in tip-top shape is to lubricate key moving parts periodically. There's definitely a Catch-22 with lubrication, however: You need to keep parts lubricated, but oil and grease attract dust. When you combine sawdust with oil or grease, you soon end up with a thick goo that can slow down parts and interfere with stops. That's why it's so important to keep your saw clean, inside and out. Before you lubricate a single part, take the time to clean first (see below). If you don't first remove the existing goo, your lubricant will be ineffective.

LUBRICATION POINTS

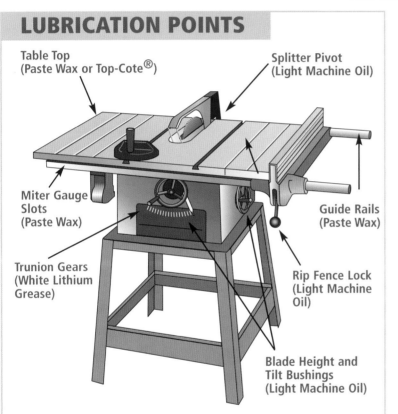

Table Top
(Paste Wax or Top-Cote®)

Splitter Pivot
(Light Machine Oil)

Miter Gauge
Slots
(Paste Wax)

Trunion Gears
(White Lithium
Grease)

Guide Rails
(Paste Wax)

Rip Fence Lock
(Light Machine
Oil)

Blade Height and
Tilt Bushings
(Light Machine Oil)

Parts outside the saw that need periodic lubrication include the saw top and miter gauge slots, the miter gauge and rip fence pivot points for locking knobs or levers, the guide rails, and the adjustment knob or wheel bushings for blade height and tilt; see the drawing at left. Inside the saw cabinet, the saw carriage, or trunion, will need lubricating; see page 134 for more on this.

Clean before you lubricate

As mentioned above, you must clean parts before lubricating them; otherwise, the fresh lubricant will not have any effect. Also, not cleaning means that dust will quickly contaminate the fresh lubricant. A shop vacuum fitted with a nozzle like the one shown in the bottom left photo will make quick work of removing dust. Take particular care in vacuuming out inside the cabinet to remove dust in all the nooks and crannies where it will hide, waiting to foul your lubricant. Trunion gears will need the attention of an old toothbrush to fully remove dirty residue from the teeth (inset below right). Clean the toothbrush frequently on a shop rag to remove excess goo. Also, pay special attention to the contact points where the blade height and tilt butt up against the stops. Built-up dust and grime here can interfere with the stops, causing them to be inaccurate (for more on these stops, see page 143).

Lubricate the blade height drive screw

Once you've vacuumed out the inside of the saw thoroughly and have cleaned all the old greasy dust from the gears, you can start applying fresh lubricant. Consult your owner's manual for recommended lubricants. If it doesn't specify any, try using white lithium grease. It's a general-purpose lubricant that will adhere well to the gears and keep them operating smoothly. Apply the fresh lubricant with a toothbrush, as shown in the top photo. Here we're applying it to the drive screw for blade height.

Lubricate the blade tilt drive screw

Next, apply a generous amount of lubricant to the drive screw for the blade tilt, as shown in the photo at right. Pack the grease into the gullets between the teeth (or screw) and wipe away any excess with a clean, dry cloth.

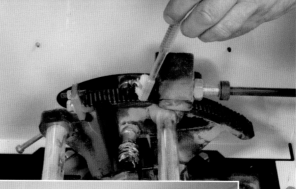

Lubricate the curved rack(s)

Now you can apply a generous amount of lubricant to the teeth of the curved racks that make contact with the blade tilt drive screw. There may be one or two of these, depending on the type of saw. Apply the lubricant with a toothbrush, as shown in the photo at right.

Lubricate bushings

The final lubrication points inside the saw are the bushings that house the shafts connecting to the blade-height and blade-tilt handwheels or knobs. On quality saws, these bushings may be bronze and require little or no lubrication; check your manual to be sure. For any metal bushings, apply a drop or two of light machine oil where the shaft exits the bushing (bottom photo). Then tilt the saw slightly and rotate the handwheel or knob to get the oil to trickle down and coat the inside of the bushing. Wipe up any excess, as light oil like this is a magnet for dust. Alternatively, consider using powdered graphite; it's harder to work into the bushing, but it doesn't attract dust.

Base and Cabinet

The base and/or cabinet is the foundation for your saw. If it's not level and not properly maintained, it can cause problems with cutting accuracy. Unfortunately, many woodworkers ignore the base/cabinet and spend considerable time and effort troubleshooting accuracy problems with no success.

Leveling a saw

With the base or cabinet attached to the saw and the saw placed in its desired location in your shop, place a level on the top from side to side and from front to back, as shown in the top photo. If your saw has leg levelers, adjust them as necessary to level the saw. If it doesn't, insert shims under the legs as necessary to make the saw level.

Dampening vibration

Vibration is one of the unseen causes of inaccurate cuts. If possible, it's usually worth the effort to bolt your saw table to the floor if the legs or cabinet are designed for this (and if you don't minding drilling holes in your floor). Alternatively, you can dampen vibration by inserting rubber anti-vibration pads under the feet; these are sold in sheets by most mail-order woodworking catalogs. Another simple way to dampen vibration is to insert a hockey puck — yes, that's right, a hockey puck — under each leg (middle photo). They're inexpensive and do a great job.

Periodic tightening

Finally, saw vibration can be caused by a base or leg assembly that's not rigid. That's why it's a good idea to periodically check and tighten any assembly bolts, as shown in the bottom photo. The ironic thing is that vibration is what usually causes the bolts to work loose in the first place. You should check your base once a month, after completing a large project that worked the saw hard, and anytime you feel that the saw is vibrating excessively. If you're using a mobile base, it's especially important to check these bolts regularly, since moving a saw about can also cause assembly bolts to loosen.

Maintaining the Table Top

Since every cut you make on a table saw involves sliding a workpiece across the top, it's important to keep the saw top maintained. In addition to helping workpieces slide smoothly, a properly maintained top will help ensure accurate cuts. Additionally, by sealing the top, you'll keep it rust-free.

Leveling the extension wings

On most table saws, the extension wings connect to the saw on one side with a set of bolts and to the guide rails on the ends. This leaves one side unsupported and, over time, gravity will tug on the wings until they sag. And when the wings sag, they can't fully support a workpiece. So regularly check to make sure the wings are level by placing a level across the top and wings, as shown in the top photo. Additionally, wings can creep out of alignment and stand proud of the saw top. This can create a ridge or lip that a workpiece can catch on, ruining a cut. If the wings are out of alignment, consult your owner's manual for the adjustment procedure.

Cleaning the top

Whenever you apply a sealer to the top to prevent rust and help workpieces glide, you should start by cleaning the top with a clean cloth dipped in solvent, such as the acetone shown in the middle photo. This will remove any old sealant or other impurities on the saw top. Always check your solvent in an inconspicuous place to make sure it won't damage the top.

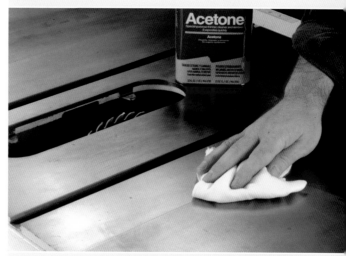

De-rusting with an abrasive pad

Once the top has been cleaned, it's good practice to follow this with an abrasive pad. Rub a pad across the entire surface of the saw top (as shown in the bottom photo) to abrade away any rust or other minor surface imperfections.

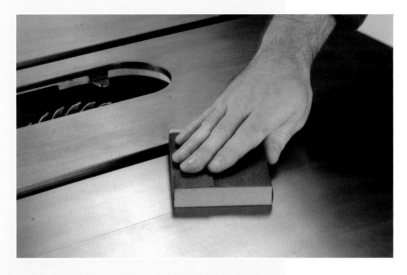

Smoothing a Top

Occasionally, you'll come across heavy rust spots or other buildups that won't come off with the abrasive pad. In cases like this, you'll need to step up to a more aggressive abrasive. Emery cloth or silicon-carbide sandpaper wrapped around a scrap block or sanding block will do a good job of leveling most buildups and removing heavy rust, see the top photo. Start with a coarse grit (such as 100), and work up to around 320-grit to remove the scratches on the top left by the prior grit. Another product that's useful here are rubber-bonded abrasive blocks sold under the Sandflex brand name (available at www.woodcraft.com). They come in fine, medium, and coarse grits and do a great job of removing rust from saw tops.

Saw top sealers: Spray on

There are a number of excellent saw top sealers available that will seal your freshly cleaned and de-rusted top. Most of these also leave a dry lubricant on the surface that promotes smooth cuts by helping workpieces glide effortlessly on the saw top. The two that we've had the most luck with are Top-Cote® and T-9 Boeshield®. Both are simply sprayed on the top, see the middle photo. Note: Before you spray, it's a good idea to thoroughly vacuum your saw top to remove any dirt, dust, or left-over sanding grit — you don't want to seal this into the top.

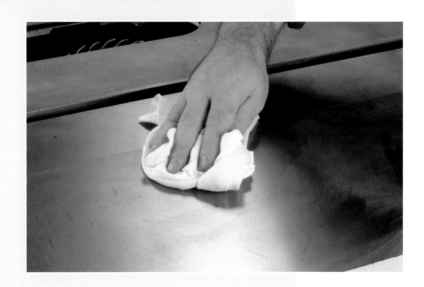

Saw top sealers: Buff off

After you've sprayed on the sealant, allow it to completely dry and then buff the saw top with a clean, dry cloth; see the bottom photo. You should see a noticeably higher sheen, and your workpieces will now glide smoothly on the saw top.

Throat Plate

The throat plate on a table saw fits in the opening in the top that lets you change blades. Most fit into a recess in the top and are simply held in place by gravity. Others are locked into the recess via a spring clip, and some rely on screws to hold the plate in place. Regardless of the holding method and plate type, all throat plates need to be flush with the saw top to prevent a workpiece from catching on the recess opening. A flush throat plate will also ensure that cuts are made with accuracy, so it won't allow a workpiece to rise and fall if it's too low or catch if it's too high.

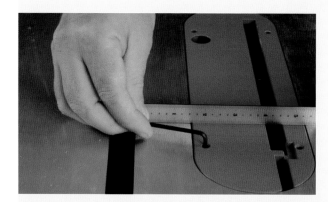

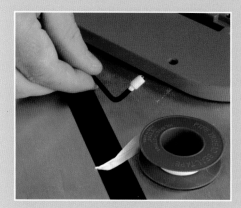

Checking a throat plate

Checking a throat plate is a simple procedure and should be done every time you remove and replace it. Simply span the throat plate with a metal rule on edge, as shown in the top right photo. Crouch down in front of the saw so your eyes are level with the saw top, and look where the rule contacts the throat plate. If you see space between the two, the plate is too low (inset). If there's space between the rule and the saw top, the plate is too high.

Adjusting a throat plate

Most, but not all, throat plates are adjustable. The most common adjustment method is a set of setscrews that contact four "tabs" inside the opening of the saw top. To adjust the throat plate, insert an Allen wrench or screwdriver into the setscrew and turn to adjust. Leave the metal rule in place and turn the setscrew until the plate just touches the rule. Once that's set, adjust the setscrew diagonal to the first one; then adjust the screw opposite the first screw and then its diagonal. Double-check the front and back and readjust as necessary until the plate is perfectly flush with the saw top.

DEALING WITH SETSCREWS

The setscrews on most throat plates have an annoying habit of vibrating out of adjustment over time. Here are a couple of quick ways to keep the setscrews locked in place.

Thread-Loc. The most common way to lock the threads of a setscrew in place is to dab a little Thread-Loc fluid onto the threads of the screw before driving it into its threaded hole. This works fine, but once dry it tends to lock the threads so tight that you have to break the bond in order to readjust if necessary.

Teflon tape. Another technique to keep setscrews from working loose is to wrap a couple turns of Teflon or plumber's tape around the screw threads. This will hold the screw tight but still allow you to readjust if necessary.

FINE-TUNING YOUR SAW TOP

Most woodworkers who've bought more than one table saw have likely learned to treat a new saw as a "kit." That's because most table saws require considerable assembly. Even the highest-quality saw will still arrive with cast or machined edges in places where these edges can do you harm, and they'll need some work to be user-friendly. Target areas for this work are the edges around the opening in the saw top, the throat plate, and the miter slots. All or any of these can have raw, jagged edges that will shred your skin.

Remove sharp edges inside the saw opening. By far the greatest hazard to skin is the metal edges of the opening in the saw top. It's not the top edges that'll usually get you (these are often machined smooth); it's the edges at the bottom of the opening. These are typically cast and not machined, and so can be rough and jagged. They'll peel the skin right off your knuckles when you go to change a blade (it doesn't help that there's little clearance in the first place, and if you have large hands, you probably skin your knuckles regularly). But it doesn't have to be like this. Grab a small mill file and file the bottom edge all the way around the opening, as shown in the top photo. Your hands will love you for it.

File the throat plate if necessary. Since you're constantly removing and replacing the throat plate, it makes sense to remove any sharp edges that can catch on your hands. Again, the problem usually isn't the top edges, but those on the bottom of the plate. Also, many throat plates don't fit easily into the saw top opening and require some force. The solution to both problems is to file the edges of the throat plate as needed, as shown in the middle photo. If the plate is too tight, file a little and check the fit. Continue like this until it slips into the opening without force.

Filing the miter gauge slots. Although the top edges of most miter gauge slots in saw tops are chamfered slightly, you'll often find (usually by drawing blood) that there are small nibs or projections on the edges of a new saw. With this in mind, consider running the flat side of a small mill file over the edges of the chamfer to knock off any nasty bits (see the bottom photo). Don't get carried away here. You don't want to remove any metal from the sides of the slots, because this can cause excessive side-to-side play in the miter gauge. If this does occur, see page 149 for some simple fixes.

Maintaining the Motor

How often your saw motor needs attention will depend primarily on what type it is. Small, sealed universal motors need little attention until they burn out. Then they must be replaced, see page 145. Larger induction motors will benefit from an occasional inspection involving the fan housing and fan, the V-belts, and pulley alignment; see below.

Keep the motor clean
Induction motors warm up with use, as current flowing through them will generate heat. Most motors have a fan blade attached to the non-drive end of the shaft to help keep the motor cool. No matter if the motor is exposed (as it is with a contractor's saw) or hidden from view (as with a cabinet saw), sawdust and chips can easily work their way into the ventilated cover that protects the fan blade. Periodically remove the fan housing, as shown in the top photo, and blow out any dust. Also, blow off accumulated dust on the blades or fins of the fan blade. Dust buildup will add a slight load to the motor and reduce the fan's cooling efficiency.

Check the pulley alignment
If your saw is belt-driven, the motor connects to the saw arbor via a V-belt and a set of pulleys. For the saw to run smoothly, the pulleys must be in line. Not only does this help reduce vibration, but it also prevents excessive wear and tear on the V-belt. To check alignment, slip a straightedge into the saw cabinet so that the straightedge is touching both edges of the saw arbor pulley as it spans the pulley. If the pulleys are in alignment, the other end of the straightedge will contact both rims of the motor pulley as it spans it; see the bottom photo and middle drawing.

Adjust if necessary
If the pulleys are out of alignment, there are a couple of ways you can adjust. One way is to loosen the setscrew that locks the motor pulley onto the motor shaft (bottom photo). Then shift the pulley in or out on the motor shaft until the pulleys align. If there's

not enough movement here to bring them into alignment, loosen the mounting bolts and shift the motor as needed.

PULLEY / SHAFT ALIGNMENT

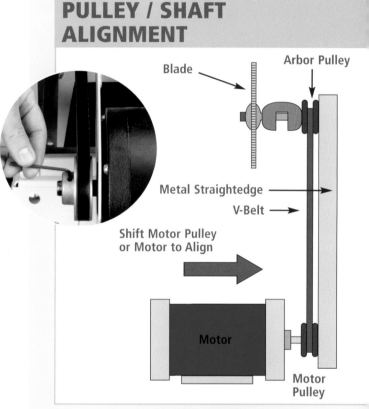

Blade

Arbor Pulley

Metal Straightedge

V-Belt

Shift Motor Pulley or Motor to Align

Motor

Motor Pulley

The Trunion

Since you depend on the table saw for accurate cuts, it's important to know how to fine-tune it so it can deliver the precision you want. What many wood-workers don't know is that a brand new table saw is often in need of fine-tuning. Unfortunately, most manuals don't mention this, leaving people frustrated and less enthusiastic for the craft. That's too bad, because tuning or aligning a table saw isn't difficult; it just takes a little know-how and some patience.

You can spend hours tweaking a miter gauge or a rip fence to get a perfect cut, but if the trunion is out of alignment, all that tweaking is just a waste of time. Regardless of whether the trunion consists of one or two parts, it's basically the carriage that holds the saw blade under the saw top and lets you adjust its height and angle, see the drawing below. A perfectly aligned trunion is the starting point for accurate cuts. Once it's aligned, you can fine-tune the other parts. Note: Don't skip this important step; if you try to align the other parts to a misaligned trunion, only headaches will result.

For your table saw to cut accurately, the blade must be parallel to the rip fence and perpendicular to the miter gauge. And it's the trunion that positions the blade with relation to the miter gauge slots and rip fence. The trunion typically attaches underneath the saw top by way of four bolts, see the drawing below. To find out whether your trunion is in alignment, see page 142. If the trunion isn't aligned, see page 143 for step-by-step instructions on how to adjust it. Also, while you're under the saw top, you may as well check the stops that position the blade at 90 degrees and 45 degrees when tilted, and the stops that set the blade height limits. See page 144 for more on checking and adjusting these stops.

TRUNION ANATOMY

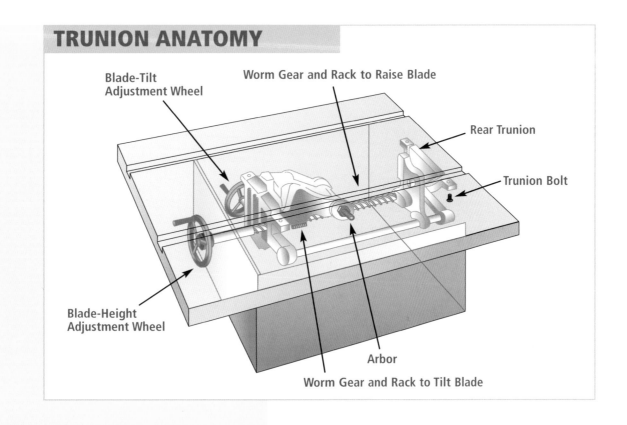

Blade-Tilt Adjustment Wheel

Worm Gear and Rack to Raise Blade

Rear Trunion

Trunion Bolt

Blade-Height Adjustment Wheel

Arbor

Worm Gear and Rack to Tilt Blade

Most methods of checking trunion alignment use the miter gauge slot as reference. A simple method is to use a combination square. Alternatively, you can build an alignment jig; see the sidebar below.

Mark the blade

To check alignment of the trunion with a combination square, first unplug the saw. Then install a blade and mark one of the teeth with a marker (top photo).

Check the leading edge

Next, rotate the blade so the "X" you marked in the previous step is positioned as far as possible toward the front of the saw and is still visible. Then press the head of a combination square firmly against the right edge of the miter gauge slot and extend the blade until it just touches the marked tooth (middle photo). Lock the blade firmly in place.

Check the trailing edge

Now rotate the blade counterclockwise so the marked tooth is at the back edge of the slot in the throat plate. Slide the combination square forward until it aligns with the marked tooth (bottom photo). Keep the head of the combination square firmly against the miter gauge slot. If the trunion is in alignment, the blade will just barely touch the tooth. If it's not in alignment, either there will be a gap between the blade and the marked tooth, or the tooth will push the blade away. If the trunion is out of alignment, see page 143 for adjustment.

ALIGNMENT JIG

A more reliable way to check alignment is with the jig shown here. The jig is a scrap of MDF that slides in the miter gauge slot. It's kerfed so a thumbscrew that threads into an insert in the bottom of the jig can lock the rod in place. To use the jig, position it across from the marked tooth and extend the rod to the tooth. Lock the rod in place with the thumbscrew, and move the jig forward and rotate the blade to check the trailing edge.

TRUNION ALIGNMENT JIG

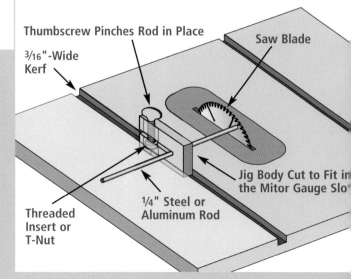

Thumbscrew Pinches Rod in Place

3/16"-Wide Kerf

Saw Blade

Jig Body Cut to Fit in the Mitor Gauge Slot

1/4" Steel or Aluminum Rod

Threaded Insert or T-Nut

ADJUSTING A TRUNION

If your trunion is out of alignment, adjusting it is fairly straightforward. What makes it a challenge is gaining access to the bolts that hold the trunion in place, since they're directly under the saw top. Additionally, the actual adjustment is really a matter of trial and error. You'll need to make an adjustment, recheck alignment, and repeat until it's aligned. You might get lucky on your first try, or it may take you an afternoon. The upside is that once you've got it adjusted and firmly lock the bolts in place, you should rarely, if ever, need to adjust the trunion again. No matter how long it takes, this is one adjustment that's well worth the effort.

Basic procedure. The basic procedure for adjusting most trunions is as follows (consult your owner's manual for specific directions for your saw). Locate and loosen the trunion mounting bolts, see the drawing below. Adjust the trunion by tapping on it, and then retighten. Check alignment, and readjust if necessary.

BLADE ALIGNMENT

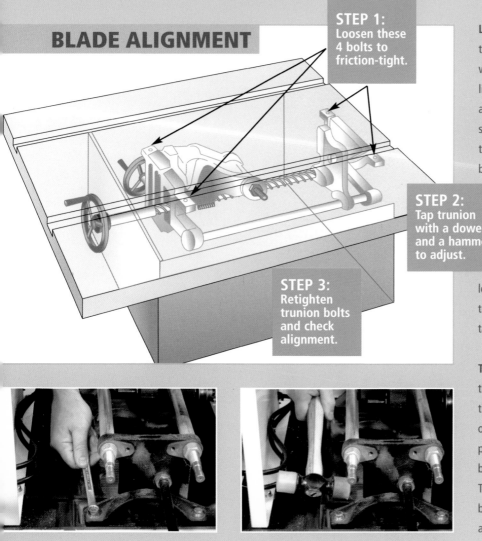

STEP 1: Loosen these 4 bolts to friction-tight.

STEP 2: Tap trunion with a dowel and a hammer to adjust.

STEP 3: Retighten trunion bolts and check alignment.

Loosen the mounting bolts. Most trunions are fairly close to alignment when they come off the assembly line. In most cases, you'll need to adjust them only a hair. One of the secrets to successfully adjusting a trunion is to loosen the mounting bolts to no more than friction-tight (bottom left photo). What this means is you loosen the bolt just enough that you can move the trunion by tapping it with a hammer. If you loosen the bolts too far, the entire trunion assembly will shift and it can take hours to get it back in place.

Tap the trunion to adjust it. With the trunion bolts loosened to friction-tight, you can adjust the position .of one or both of the trunions by tapping them with a soft-faced or dead-blow hammer (bottom right photo). Tap in tiny increments, retighten the bolts, and recheck alignment. Repeat as necessary.

All trunions have stops to limit how high the blade can be raised and how far it can tilt. All of these can be off on a brand-new saw and will often vibrate out of adjustment over time. The stops on most trunions are adjustable. The stops that you'll most often need to adjust are those used for blade tilt. Blade height rarely calls for adjustment, as it's set at the factory and shouldn't be tampered with: It's adjusted to match maximum cut with the motor's power. Trying to tweak this stop to get a little more blade height can over-work the motor and cause it to burn out prematurely.

Check the 90-degree stop

Raise the blade fully and turn the blade-tilt handwheel or knob until it hits the 90-degree stop. Then butt a small try square (an engi-neer's square like the one shown in the inset photo is perfect for this) up against the saw blade, taking care that it doesn't hit any teeth. If the square does not rest perfectly flush with the saw blade, the 90-degree stop is out of alignment.

Adjust the 90-degree stop

The adjustment for the 90-degree stop is on the front trunion on most saws. It's typically a machine bolt held in place with a jam nut. Loosen the nut and adjust the stop with an Allen wrench, screw-driver, or socket wrench (top photo). Tighten the jam nut, recheck alignment, and repeat as necessary.

Check the 45-degree stop

You can check the 45-degree stop by tilting the blade until it hits the stop. Then insert the head of a combination square between the blade and table top, as shown in the middle photo. Check for a gap between the head and the saw blade.

Adjust the 45-degree stop

The 45-degree stop is usually located at the side of the front trunion, as shown in the bottom photo. It also is typically a machine bolt locked in place with a jam nut. Loosen the jam nut, adjust the setscrew, and retighten. Check alignment again and adjust as necessary.

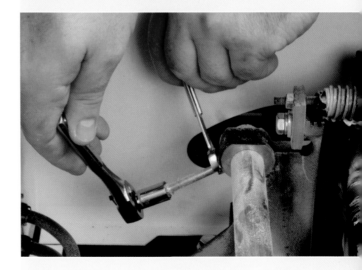

Electrical Repairs

The electrical system of a table saw is simple and straightforward. Power enters through the plug and continues up the electrical cord. On its way to the motor it passes through the on/off switch, which serves to control the flow. Any of these components can be replaced fairly easily using the manufacturer's replacement part.

Replacing a cord

How readily you can replace an electrical cord depends mostly on the manufacturer. On some saws you have to crawl under the saw or flip it over to access the power connections. Other manufacturers offer detachable housings that provide relatively easy access. In any case, once the ends of the cord are in sight, make a note of wire colors, locations, and routing. Replace the cord by removing one wire at a time and installing the matching wire of the new cord (upper left photo). This way there won't be any wiring mistakes.

Replacing a power switch

The complexity of replacing a power switch on a table saw will depend on the manufacturer and on the type of switch you're replacing. Switches vary from simple toggle switches to more advanced magnetic ones. To replace a switch, remove the cover plate and gently pull out the switch. Then note the wire colors and locations before removing the old switch. The most reliable way to replace any power switch is to disconnect one wire at a time and connect it to the corresponding terminal on the replacement switch (see the inset photo above).

Replacing a motor

The type of saw will determine how tough or easy it is to replace a defective motor. Contractor's saws are the easiest, as the motor is fully exposed at the rear of the saw. Lift the motor to disconnect the drive belt, loosen and remove the motor mounting bolts, and set aside. Reverse this to install the new motor. Titling-arbor saws are the next easiest, as they are also belt-driven. The only challenge here is lack of elbow room inside the cabinet. Bench-top saws are the most difficult since you'll basically have to gut the insides of the saw to remove the direct-drive universal motor — and there's little room (lower photo). One tip that will help with reassembly is to thread screws back into the holes that they came from as you remove parts. This helps you keep track of the many parts. Also, have the exploded view diagram from your owner's manual on hand to serve as a visual reference.

Maintaining the Rip Fence

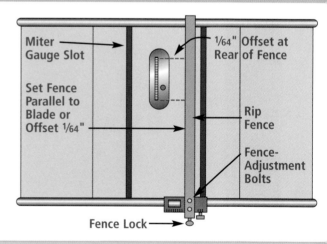

One of the most common causes of problems making cuts on the table saw is an improperly aligned rip fence. Not only can this cause inaccurate cuts, but it also can pinch a workpiece between the fence and blade, causing binding, burning, and kickback. The good news is it's easy to both check and align your rip fence — as long as your trunion is in alignment (see pages 141–144 for more on this). Make sure it is before you spend any time adjusting your fence.

Check rip fence alignment
When a rip fence is properly aligned, it's parallel to the saw blade or offset slightly; see below. As long as your trunion is aligned, and you used the miter gauge slots to align it, you can use these slots to align the rip fence. The rip fence, the miter gauge slots, and the saw blades should all be parallel to each other. With this in mind, you can check rip fence alignment by simply sliding the fence over until one edge is aligned with one side of the miter gauge slot. Lock the rip fence in place and gently run your finger along the inside edge of the miter gauge slot, as shown in the above photo. The edge of the fence and the side of the slot should be flush; if they're not, adjust the fence as described on page 147.

OFFSET RIP FENCE

Some woodworkers prefer to angle the top end of their rip fence away from the saw blade a tiny bit to help prevent binding. Typically, they'll adjust the rip fence to be from 1/64" to 1/16" away from parallel (drawing at right). Offset can be checked and adjusted by placing a metal rule against the fence and measuring the offset at a miter gauge slot (photo below). If your trunion is aligned, this generally should not be necessary.

But if you're planning on sawing a lot of green wood, or wood that's not completely dry, you may want to consider offsetting your fence. That's because wood that isn't completely dry tends to move considerably as it's cut. The ends of a green board will often splay apart as soon as a kerf is created by the blade. When this happens, the splayed ends can push the board away from the rip fence, causing it to bind and burn. Offset will help prevent this. As long as you feed stock into the blade by pressing it against the infeed portion of the rip fence, you shouldn't have any problems with accuracy. Problems do arise, however, when you feed stock and angle the board to keep it in contact with the outfeed portion of the rip fence. If you do this with an offset fence, you'll end up with a board that doesn't have parallel edges.

RIP FENCE ALIGNMENT

Miter Gauge Slot

Set Fence Parallel to Blade or Offset 1/64"

1/64" Offset at Rear of Fence

Rip Fence

Fence-Adjustment Bolts

Fence Lock ➤

Alignment: Loosen mounting screws or bolts

If your rip fence is out of alignment or you want to add some offset, start by loosening the rip fence mounting bolts to friction-tight, as shown in the top photo. There are almost always two of these, and they may be bolts or machine screws with hex heads, slotted heads, or heads that accept an Allen wrench. Take care here to loosen them only enough to adjust the fence with a hammer, see below.

Alignment: Tap to adjust

With the rip fence bolts loosened to friction-tight, tap the end of the fence with a soft-faced or dead-blow hammer on the side that you want to angle it away from (middle photo). Tap lightly here and then check the alignment. If it's good, tighten the bolts and check one more time; tightening the bolts can often rack the fence out of alignment. If it's not aligned, tap again and repeat as necessary until it comes into alignment. Then retighten the bolts to lock the aligned fence in place.

Alignment: Check for perpendicular to top

While you're checking the fence, it's also a good idea to test it to make sure the face of the fence is parallel to the saw top — something that's imperative for a square edge cut. Although you may not notice a misaligned fence when cutting thin stock, it'll be more obvious with thicker stock and particularly when you cut tenons on the ends of boards. To check alignment, just butt a try square up against the fence as shown in the bottom photo. There should be no gap between the square and the fence or the saw top. If there is, you'll need to correct this. Check your owner's manual for adjustment procedure. In most cases you'll have to shim the fence to bring it into alignment.

Maintaining the Miter Gauge

Next to your rip fence, the miter gauge is the second most-used guide for making cuts on the table saw. As with the rip fence, it makes no sense at all to spend time aligning it if your trunion isn't aligned. (See pages 141–144 for step-by-step directions on how to check and align your trunion.) But alignment does not guarantee accurate crosscuts — the miter gauge must slide smoothly back and forth in the slots with little or no play. If your miter gauge does exhibit any side-to-side play, there are a couple of simple remedies for this; see page 149. If there is play in your miter gauge, remove any play first before checking alignment.

Checking the alignment

A quick way to check miter gauge alignment is to use a try square. Butt the handle of a square up against the head of the miter gauge and slide it over until the blade butts up against the saw blade, as shown in the upper photo at right. Make sure to rotate the saw blade so the ends of the saw blade press up against the try square blade, not the carbide tips. Then loosen the miter gauge handle to friction-tight and adjust the position of the miter gauge head until the blade of the try square butts squarely up against the saw blade. Tighten the miter gauge handle and adjust the 90-degree stop, see below.

Adjusting the stops

Once you have your miter gauge aligned for true 90-degree cuts, take the time to set the 90-degree stop. On most miter gauges, this is just a machine screw locked in place with a jam nut. The end of the machine screw butts up against a lever that pivots out of the way when you need to adjust the gauge. Before you make the adjustment, check to make sure the lever is straight. If it's bent, straighten it with a pair of locking-jaw pliers. Then loosen the jam nut to friction-tight and

gently rotate the screw until it just contacts the lever, see the bottom left photo. Tighten the jam nut and check alignment once more, in case tightening the nut affected the screw position. Repeat this procedure for the 45-degree stops, using a combination or speed square as your 45-degree reference.

Make some test cuts

After you've adjusted the stops, make a couple of crosscuts on some wide stock. Then use a try square with a long blade or a framing square to check the ends for square, as shown in the bottom right photo. If the ends aren't perfectly square, repeat the alignment procedure, readjust the stop, and try again.

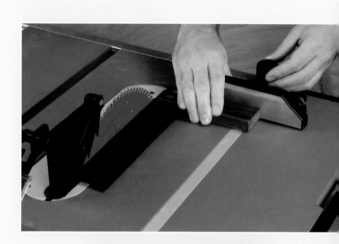

REMOVING PLAY FROM A MITER GAUGE

One of the most common causes of inaccurate crosscuts is a miter gauge that doesn't fit tightly in the slots in the saw top. Just a tiny bit of play here can cause a 1- to 4-degree error in the end angle of a board, depending on its width.

Checking for excessive play. To determine whether there's any side-to-side play in your miter gauge, set the miter gauge in one of the slots in the saw top. Then grip the handle of the miter gauge lightly and try to wiggle it from side to side, as shown in the top photo. You'll both hear and feel any play. Repeat this for the other miter gauge slot.

If you detect play, there are two simple ways to remove it: by dimpling the bar of the miter gauge or by applying metal tape, as discussed below.

Removing play with dimples. One way to remove side-to-side play of a miter gauge is to dimple the miter gauge bar, as shown in the middle photo. What dimpling does is create tiny raised crater-shaped ridges in the side of the bar. Dimples can be made with a centerpunch and a hammer. The harder you strike the punch, the more you will raise the sides of the dimple. Start by striking a series of small dimples in the side of the bar. Work only where you know there's excessive play. Slip the miter gauge in the slot and check for side-to-side movement. What you're after here is a trade-off between no play and smooth movement. Increase the size of the dimples if necessary to remove play, or try dimpling the other side. If the bar gets too tight in the slot, knock the high points off the dimples with a block of wood wrapped in emery cloth.

Removing play with metal tape. Another option for removing excessive play is to apply metal foil tape to one or both sides of the miter gauge bar, as shown in the bottom photo. Metal foil tape can be found in the heating and cooling aisle in most home centers and hardware stores. It's used to seal the joints between connecting metal ducting. Because it's metal, it will hold up well to the wear and tear. Cut a strip to width, peel off the backing, and apply it to the side of the bar. If necessary, apply a strip or two to the opposite side until the side-to-side play is gone.

Maintaining Blades

Saw blades need regular maintenance. Although carbide-tipped blades require much less frequent sharpening than high-speed steel (HSS) blades, both types will cut truer and last longer if stored properly and kept clean.

Storing blades

The number one thing you can do to increase the life of your saw blades is to store them properly when they're not being used. Proper storage includes replacing a blade in its original packaging, as shown in the top photo, or setting blades in a simple storage rack, like the one shown on page 42. Both of these methods keep the teeth from coming in contact with metal. The worst thing you can do is allow blades to lie on top of one another or hang them on a wall. When teeth touch, they dull (if high-speed steel) or fracture or chip (if carbide-tipped).

Cleaning setup

With use, saw blades will pick up pitch and gum from the woods you cut. If you cut a lot of softwoods, the blades can pick up a lot of resin as well. Any of these buildups on your saw blades will decrease the cutting efficiency of the blades and also tend to cause burning and ragged cuts. To promote blade cleaning, consider making a blade-cleaning kit consisting of an old or disposable pizza pan, an old toothbrush, rubber gloves, and a can of pitch and gum remover, as shown in the middle photo. Keep a couple of old newspapers on hand as well to protect surrounding work surfaces.

Brush your teeth

To clean a blade, put on a pair of rubber gloves and place the blade in the pizza pan. Spray on a coat of pitch and gum remover, and wait the recommended time. After it has set, scrub the teeth with an old toothbrush to remove stubborn deposits, as shown in the bottom photo. Wipe off any excess with the clean cloth, flip the blade, and clean the other side. When done, wipe both sides and clean one

more time. If rust is a problem in your shop, consider spraying on a sealer such as Dri-Cote to keep out harmful moisture.

Deburr the arbor hole if necessary

Constant blade changing can create burrs around the arbor hole of a saw blade. These form when the blade strikes the arbor as you repeatedly try to align the arbor hole with the arbor. Eventually these burrs will make it difficult to install or remove the blade. So every time you clean a blade, stop and check for burrs. Just run your fingertip lightly around the arbor hole. If you find any burrs, remove them with a half-round file as shown in the top photo. Warning: Do not alter the diameter of the hole, as this will make the blade wobble. File only on the surface of the blade, not within the hole.

Sharpening carbide-tipped blades

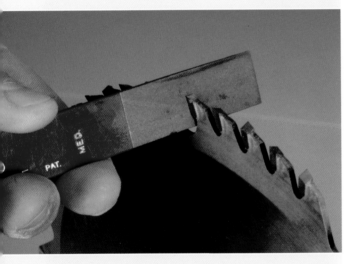

Carbide-tipped blades are best sharpened by a professional who has experience working with carbide. If you don't know of a local sharpener, consult a local woodworking club if there is one in your area. Don't use a sharpening service that has not been recommended by a woodworker. If the shop doesn't have the specialized equipment needed to hone a carbide-tipped blade, they can ruin it. And with most blades costing over $100, you would not be happy. Alternatively, some blade manufacturers and mail-order woodworking suppliers offer sharpening service. If you notice a chip or a slightly dull tooth, you can freshen the edge by filing the flats with a diamond hone (middle photo). Note: This is only for a tooth or two; leave the sharpening to a pro.

Sharpening high-speed steel blades

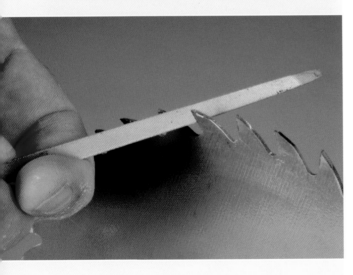

Just like any other high-speed steel blade in your workshop (like a plane or handsaw blade), an HSS saw blade can be sharpened with a slim taper file like the one shown in the bottom photo. Here again, we advise you to have this done professionally because if you don't sharpen every tooth identically and set each alternate tooth perfectly, the blade will not run true. It can pull to one side or, if one or more teeth protrude even slightly, they'll do all the cutting and dull quickly, leaving a jagged cut. Touch-up sharpening can be done by pressing a file against the tooth so it aligns with the bevel. Then take one or two passes with the file to create a fresh edge.

■ TROUBLESHOOTING

Because there are so many parts and adjustments on a table saw, there is a lot of room for error — and problems. The next six pages are devoted to common problems and their solutions, including: inaccurate rip cuts and crosscuts, burning, stepped shoulders, and saws that bog down during a cut.

INACCURATE RIP CUTS

Since ripping is one of the primary functions of a table saw and these cuts often form the building blocks of a project, a saw that can't rip accurately is a big problem (inset photo).

Rip fence out of alignment. The primary cause of inaccurate rip cuts is a rip fence out of alignment (top right photo). See pages 146–147 for step-by-step directions on how to check and align your rip fence.

Trunion out of alignment. If the rip fence is aligned but the trunion is not, your ripping will not be accurate. That's because when the trunion is out of alignment, the blade will not be parallel to the rip fence; it will either angle in or angle away from the fence. See pages 141–144 for directions on how to check and adjust the trunion (middle photo).

Fence lock not positive. Finally, rip cuts that are off can be caused by a bad or improperly adjusted rip fence lock (bottom photo). Even if the rip fence starts out parallel at the start of the cut, a loose fence lock can allow you to push the fence out of alignment as you press the workpiece into the rip fence. To check this, lock down the fence and push against it with the heel of your hand. If it moves, it needs to be tightened. Adjustment will depend on your saw; consult the owner's manual.

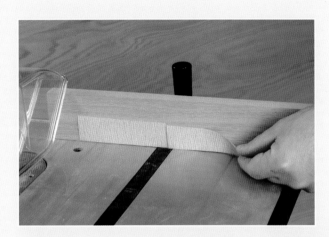

INACCURATE CROSSCUTS

Crosscuts that end up jagged or the wrong angle (inset photo) can be caused by a number of things, all centered around the miter gauge. Problems tend to be exacerbated by long or wide stock. Long stock in particular wants to wobble and tilt, so it's important to use an auxiliary fence like the one shown on page 55 and some kind of auxiliary side support (either a roller or support stand or a nearby bench or two, as described on page 47).

Workpiece creeping. Because a saw blade tends to pull or push a workpiece when cross-cutting, you'll need to take some precautions to prevent this. One of the simplest ways is to apply a couple of strips of self-adhesive sandpaper to the face of your auxiliary fence, as shown in the top left photo. The grit will help "grab" the workpiece and keep it from shifting during a cut.

Stop blocks not being used. Another way to help keep a workpiece from shifting during a crosscut is to add a stop block to your auxiliary fence, as shown in the middle photo. A stop block also makes it easy to make repeat cuts with precision (see page 56 for more on working with stop blocks).

Stops not aligned properly. Finally, if the miter gauge stops are not adjusted properly, you'll have problems cutting accurate 90-degree and 45-degree crosscuts. See page 148 for step-by-step directions on how to align and adjust the miter gauge stops (bottom photo).

BURNING

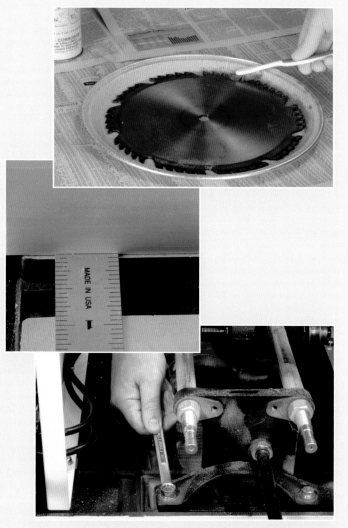

A table saw that burns the wood during a cut needs immediate attention (inset). Burns are caused by excess friction between the wood and the blade. There are a number of reasons this occurs, and the simplest is operator error: You're moving the wood past the blade too slowly — you need to increase your feed rate. If this doesn't solve the problem, see below.

Blade is dirty or dull. A dirty or dull blade causes burning because pitch and gum build up on the teeth and the teeth can't cut cleanly (top right photo). See pages 150–151 for instructions on how to clean and sharpen your blades.

Rip fence out of alignment. If the rip fence is out of alignment and angles in toward the saw blade, it'll pinch the workpiece between the fence and the blade and the wood will burn (middle photo). See pages 146–147 for directions on how to check and adjust your rip fence.

Trunion may be out of alignment. If neither of the above solutions fixes your burning problem, the trunion may be out of alignment (bottom photo at right). Find instructions for checking and adjusting the trunion on pages 141–144.

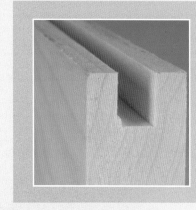

STEPPED SHOULDERS

Stepped shoulders (where the bottom of a cut isn't flat or the sides of a tenon aren't flush) can be caused by a couple of things (see photo at left). First, make sure the throat plate is adjusted flush with the saw top (see page 138). Second, check to make sure your rip fence is perpendicular to the saw top (see page 147). And finally, be sure to use consistent pressure when you make multiple-pass cuts. Easing up on a workpiece will let it rise up, leaving an uneven bottom. Featherboards can help to prevent this (see page 33.)

RAGGED CUTS

Cuts that aren't clean are a common problem in many woodshops (inset). Most of the time, ragged cuts can be prevented with a few simple measures. It's important to realize that some wood species and grain configurations tend to tear or leave ragged cuts regardless of what you do to prevent it. Species that tend to not cut cleanly are elm and mesquite; oily exotics like teak also can cause problems because they're very abrasive and will quickly dull your blade, producing a ragged cut. Wood grain configurations such as bird's-eye, fiddleback, and tiger stripe leave much to be desired when cutting, as the grain direction fluctuates wildly; odds are you'll be cutting with and against the grain in a single cut.

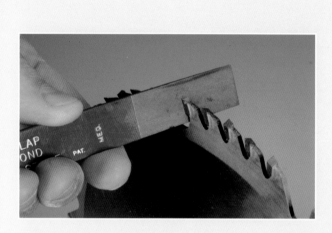

Blade may be dull or dirty. If you're experiencing ragged cuts on woods that aren't finicky (like most straight-grained domestic hardwoods and softwoods), the first thing to look at is your blade (top left photo). A dull or dirty blade will not cut cleanly. See pages 150–151 on how to maintain blades.

Backer boards not being used. Another form of a ragged cut, chip-out, will result if you make a cross-grain cut (either a full crosscut or a dado or groove) without using a backer board (middle photo). A backer board supports the wood fibers of the workpiece as the blade exits the trailing edge. Chip-out still occurs on the backer board, but it's scrap wood and besides, that's what it's there for.

Trunion out of alignment. An out-of-alignment trunion can cause a ragged cut, as the blade will be at an angle to the rip fence and miter gauge. Either the leading or the trailing edge of the workpiece will come in contact with the angled teeth, resulting in a poor cut (bottom photo). See pages 141–144 for information on checking and aligning the trunion.

SAW BOGS DOWN

So you're happily cutting wood in your shop and suddenly the saw bogs down. You can hear it because the tone of the saw motor drops, and you feel it because it's harder to feed the wood into the saw. What's happening here is that friction (from one source or another) is loading down the saw blade and motor. When this occurs, stop and turn off the saw. Allow the blade to come to a complete stop and then remove the workpiece. If you continue cutting, the motor will draw more power and can blow a fuse or circuit breaker. If by chance you have a high-amperage line running to the saw (say, a 30-amp line for a motor that requires 20 amps), you can overheat and damage the motor.

Feed rate too fast. In many instances, the only reason a saw bogs down is that you're trying to feed stock into it too fast (top photo). This is particularly noticeable on bench-top saws with universal motors. Try reducing your feed rate. If you find that burning occurs, pick up the rate a bit. If you have to slow the feed rate down so far that burning occurs, consider making the cut in two passes (see page 51).

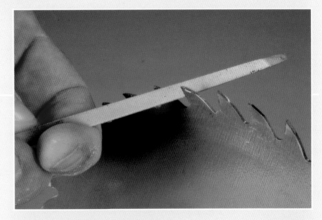

Blade is dull or dirty. You've no doubt figured out by now that a dull or dirty blade can cause many of the problems associated with a poor cut. See pages 150–151 for more on cleaning and sharpening saw blades (middle photo at right).

Motor is underpowered. A saw that bogs down may be telling you that you're trying to bite off more than it can chew. Bench-top saws (bottom photo) typically have small universal motors, and these just can't handle some of the more stout cuts that a larger saw can handle, like cutting through 3"-thick white oak. Your only solutions here are to make the cut in two passes if possible, have a friend with a beefier saw cut it for you, or upgrade to a more powerful saw.

Casehardened wood. Another reason a saw will bog down is if you happen to be cutting casehardened wood. Casehardening is a result of improper drying techniques and cannot be detected without cutting into a board. The problem arises because of the difference in moisture content between the exterior and interior of the wood. When casehardened wood is cut, internal stresses can force the kerf apart — or more usually together, like the board shown in the top photo. When the kerf closes, it will pinch the splitter and blade. It can close with such force that it can bring the blade on a 3-hp cabinet saw to a dead stop. Unfortunately, there is no fix for this problem. Just turn off your saw and pitch the wood in the trash pile or burn bin. If you've bought a lot of this wood, contact your lumber supplier. A reputable dealer will replace the wood or refund your money.

Saw top is not smooth and clean. Wood can bog down a saw if it catches on the saw top. A dull or dirty top can create a surprising amount of drag on a workpiece; the resulting friction can bog down the saw. See pages 136–137 for directions on how to keep your saw top clean and smooth (upper left photo).

Rip fence is out of alignment. Finally, a rip fence that's out of alignment can bog down a saw. If the rip fence is angled in toward the blade, it'll pinch the workpiece between the blade and splitter, resulting in friction that'll slow the motor. See pages 146–147 for information on how to check and adjust your rip fence (bottom photo at left).

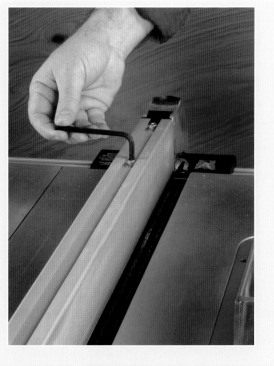

7 Table Saw Projects

The table saw is such a versatile machine that you can craft many projects with it alone. This chapter features five projects that not only produce attractive furniture, but also give you the chance to try some new techniques. For example, the demilune table on pages 160–164 has legs that are tapered with a shop-made taper jig (pages 126–129), and curved aprons that use a technique called kerf-bending (pages 92–93). The leg parts of the blanket chest showcased on pages 170–175 are glued up using a mitered spline joint. Then, stub-tenon-and-groove joinery is used to join these legs to the sides, front, and back. The bookcase shown on pages 165–169 is an excellent exercise in cutting dadoes, grooves, and rabbets — as well as miters. What's better is that you end up with a good-looking and very sturdy bookcase.

The photo on the opposite page shows just one of the five table saw projects featured in this chapter. It's a sturdy but earnest occasional table inspired by the Arts & Crafts movement. Although it does have open mortise-and-tenon construction, no mortises or tenons need to be cut; see pages 184–189 to learn how this is possible.

Demilune Table

A demilune table gets its name from the half-moon shape of its top. It is also referred to as a bow-front table, D-shaped table, half-round table, pier table, or semicircular table. Whatever you call it, this classic table will grace any home. Its narrow width makes it the perfect table for a hallway or entryway. Demilune tables often have four legs, but we chose to simplify construction by using only three legs.

The legs on most demilune tables are tapered like the ones on this table. We used the shop-made taper jig shown on pages 126–129 to taper the legs. The big challenge to making this table is the curved-front apron. The simplest way to curve wood for this is to cut a series of relief kerfs in the back of the apron. The kerfing jig shown on pages 92–93 is perfect for this job.

We used red oak for this table, but any hardwood will do — walnut looks particularly nice. The table top is made of ³/₄" matching plywood, and the edges are covered with veneer tape, although you could make it from solid wood.

MATERIALS LIST

Part	Quantity	Dimensions
Legs	3	1¹/₂" × 28" – 1¹/₂"
Bending forms	2	13" × 35" – ³/₄" plywood
Aprons	2	4" × 22¹/₂"* – ³/₄" plywood
Spacer blocks	3	1¹/₂" × 2¹/₂" – 1¹/₂"
Top	1	14³/₄" × 38" – ³/₄" plywood
Top edging	1	³/₄"-wide veneer
*cut to fit		

EXPLODED VIEW

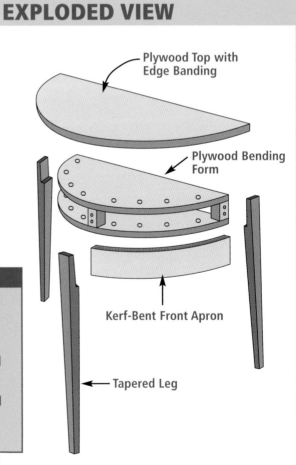

Plywood Top with Edge Banding

Plywood Bending Form

Kerf-Bent Front Apron

Tapered Leg

Taper the legs

To make the demilune table, start by cutting the leg stock to length and width. Then drill a $1/4$"-diameter hole in one end of each leg to fit onto the index pin of the taper jig shown on pages 126–129. Fit a leg onto the taper jig via the index pin, and adjust the jig for the desired taper as shown on the leg side view on page 162. The taper begins 5" from the top of the leg. Position the rip fence to make the cut, and push the taper jig and workpiece past the blade (top photo).

Use a push stick to press the opposite end of the workpiece against the jig as you make the cut (see the top photo on page 126). When the first taper is cut, turn off the saw, return the jig to its starting position, and rotate the workpiece to present the next leg face to the blade. Turn on the saw and cut as you did for the first pass (middle photo at left). The index pin will hold the workpiece perfectly centered for the cut. Repeat for the other two sides and the remaining legs. Remove any saw marks with a hand plane or sanding block.

Make the bending forms

Once the legs are tapered, you can make the bending forms that the kerf-bent aprons are wrapped around. A simple way to lay out the half-moon shape is to draw a gravity curve. To make a gravity curve, drape a chain or string from one end of the bending form to the other, starting 2" down from the back edge of the plywood. Drape the chain or string so that the bottom of the arch hits the center of the board; then carefully trace around the string/chain (inset at near left). Now cut out the bending form and use this to mark out the second form; cut this to shape (bottom left photo). Clamp the forms together and sand or file the edges smooth.

Drill clamping holes for the aprons

The kerf-bent aprons are attached to the bending forms with glue. The aprons are held in place with clamps while the glue dries. In order to apply even pressure, you'll need to drill holes in the forms for the clamp heads. These holes, eight on each form, are 2" in from the edge of the forms and spaced every 5" to 6" apart. Lay these out by setting a compass 2" wide. Then place the point against the edge of the curved form and slide the compass along the edge to scribe a curve 2" in from the edge. Mark the holes on the curve, and then use a $1^1/4$" spade bit or Forstner bit to drill the holes (top photo).

Attach spacer blocks to the forms

Three spacer blocks are sandwiched between the bending forms to space them apart, one block at each end and one centered on the front edge. The legs also attach to these blocks. To make it easier to mount the legs later, drill a centered pilot hole in each block $1/2$" down from both edges before you attach them to the forms. Butt a scrap of plywood against the back (flat) edges of the forms to keep them aligned. Also, use a try square to make sure the front edges are flush. Attach each block to the forms with two #6 × $1^1/2$" woodscrews on each end (middle photo).

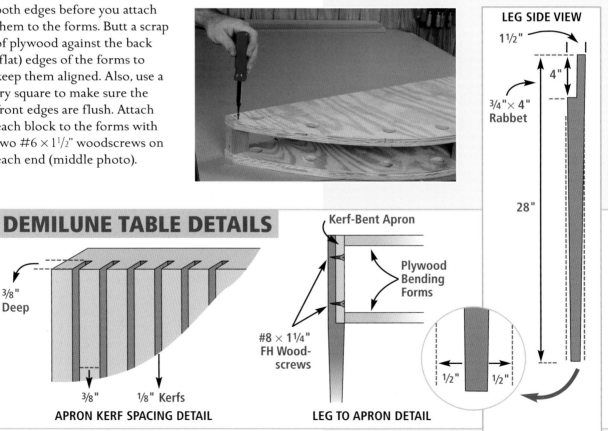

DEMILUNE TABLE DETAILS

3/8" Deep

3/8"   1/8" Kerfs

APRON KERF SPACING DETAIL

Kerf-Bent Apron

Plywood Bending Forms

#8 × 1¼" FH Woodscrews

LEG TO APRON DETAIL

1/2"   1/2"

LEG SIDE VIEW

1½"

4"

3/4" × 4" Rabbet

28"

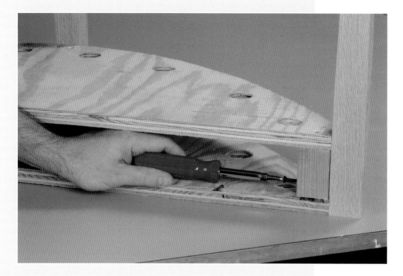

Attach the legs to the spacer blocks

The legs are attached to the spacer blocks with a pair of #10 × 2½" wood-screws. Butt each leg up against a spacer block and clamp it in place so it's plumb; use a try square to verify this, then attach it with screws, as shown in the top photo. The legs on the ends are easy, as you can just reach inside the back to tighten the screws. The center leg is trickier: Because it's so far from the back edge, it's hard to get a screwdriver in between the forms. A drill bit extension for your electric drill fitted with a screw-driver bit is one way to handle this. Another is to use hex-head screws and drive them in with a socket wrench from the front of the bending forms.

Cut the apron blanks to width

With the legs in place, you can cut the apron pieces to width and o rough length. Rip two ¾"-thick plywood aprons to a width of 4" and to a rough length of 24", as shown in the middle photo. Make sure to cut these with the good face up to reduce splintering of the thin face veneer.

Kerf the aprons

In order for the aprons to bend around the forms, they need to be kerfed. Use the kerfing jig described on pages 92–93 for this. Attach the jig to your miter gauge for ¼" kerf spacing. Make a couple of test kerfs to ensure that the spacing is correct. Then use the miter gauge to push the project piece past the blade as shown in the bottom photo. Return the miter gauge to its starting position and lift the work-piece; slip the kerf you just cut over the index pin. Cut another kerf and repeat this process until all the kerfs are cut. Make sure to press the workpiece flat against the saw top as you make each cut, since the kerfed piece will tend to bow up slightly as it's kerfed. Pressing down keeps all the webs the same thickness and ensures a smooth bend. Note: Once kerfed, the apron blanks will be fragile and can break easily. Handle them gently until they're attached to the bending forms.

Attach the aprons to the forms

Now you're ready to attach the aprons to the bending forms. Because the ends of the aprons butt up against the legs at angles, you'll need to angle the ends for a good fit. Hold the apron blank up against the leg while pressing it against the forms. Approximate the angle and cut the end; adjust as necessary. When you've got one end fit, angle-cut the other end. Start long here and sneak up on the final fit. Repeat for the other apron. Then, working on one apron at a time, apply glue generously to the edges of the forms, set the apron in place, and secure with clamps, as shown in the top photo.

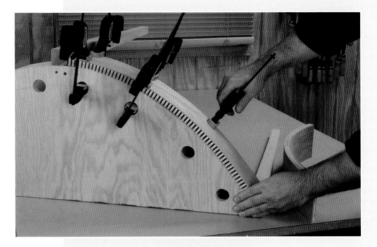

Make the top

After the aprons have dried, you can make the top. Set the table upside down on the bottom of the top blank. Then trace around the aprons with a compass set $^3/_4$" wide; stop when you hit each leg. Remove the table and complete the curve by connecting the sections you just scribed. Cut the top to shape with a saber saw or band saw, as shown in the middle photo

at right. Sand the edges smooth and then cover the exposed plywood edges with veneer tape. The pre-glued variety that we used here is applied with an iron (inset at left). When the tape cools, sand the edges smooth. Alternatively, you can make the top from solid wood.

Attach the top to the table

To complete the demilune table, place the top onto the table so there's an even overlap on the front edge; secure it with #8 × 1$^1/_4$" woodscrews (bottom photo at right). Use the clamp-head holes in the bending forms for access. Drive the screws up through these holes, through the bending form, and into the top.

Bookcase

This sturdy yet simple-to-build bookcase has all-around appeal: It's the perfect project for a beginning woodworker, yet people of all skill levels will appreciate its solid construction and classic lines. The carcase of the bookcase is made entirely out of $3/4$" hardwood plywood (we used red oak). A simple mitered face frame and shelf supports cover the exposed plywood edges, and also help create a more rigid unit. The top is made of plywood as well, and is edged with $3/4$" solid stock.

The two lower shelves are spaced to accept most books, and the upper shelf will hold paperbacks. But you can custom-position them by simply cutting the dadoes that support the shelf ends anywhere you want.

EXPLODED VIEW

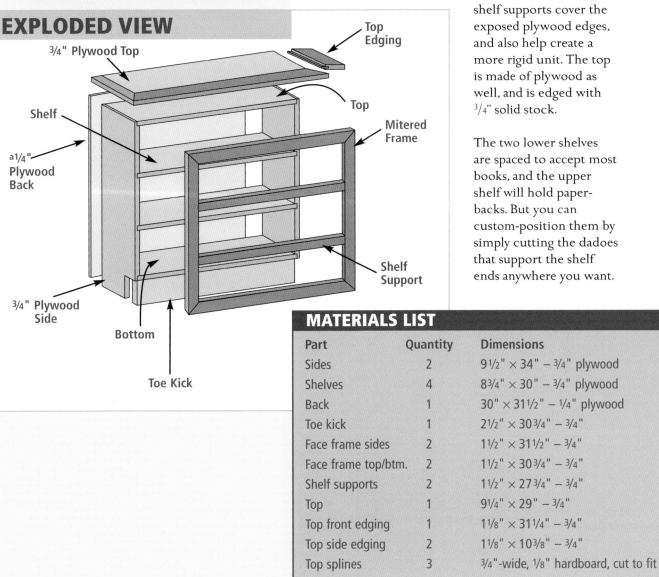

$3/4$" Plywood Top

Top Edging

Shelf

a$1/4$" Plywood Back

Top

Mitered Frame

Shelf Support

$3/4$" Plywood Side

Bottom

Toe Kick

MATERIALS LIST

Part	Quantity	Dimensions
Sides	2	$9\,1/2$" × 34" – $3/4$" plywood
Shelves	4	$8\,3/4$" × 30" – $3/4$" plywood
Back	1	30" × $31\,1/2$" – $1/4$" plywood
Toe kick	1	$2\,1/2$" × $30\,3/4$" – $3/4$"
Face frame sides	2	$1\,1/2$" × $31\,1/2$" – $3/4$"
Face frame top/btm.	2	$1\,1/2$" × $30\,3/4$" – $3/4$"
Shelf supports	2	$1\,1/2$" × $27\,3/4$" – $3/4$"
Top	1	$9\,1/4$" × 29" – $3/4$"
Top front edging	1	$1\,1/8$" × $31\,1/4$" – $3/4$"
Top side edging	2	$1\,1/8$" × $10\,3/8$" – $3/4$"
Top splines	3	$3/4$"-wide, $1/8$" hardboard, cut to fit

Cut rabbets and dadoes in the sides

Start work on the bookshelf by cutting the sides to size (see the exploded view and materials list on page 165). The shelves of the bookcase fit into dadoes and rabbets cut into the sides (see the detail drawings on page 167). Install a dado set in the saw and position the rip fence as a stop, as shown in the top photo. Both the dadoes and the rabbets are sized to fit $3/4$" plywood. Install shims in the dado set as necessary to get a snug fit. All of these are $3/8$" deep. Make a book-matched pair of sides, with the good face of the plywood facing out on both sides.

Notch the front corner of each side

The bottom front corner of each side is notched to provide toe room. The toe kick is attached to the front edges of this notch later. The notch is $2^1/2$" square and can be cut with a saber saw, as shown in the middle photo, or on the band saw. Take care to make the notch cuts such that you end up with a pair of book-matched sides. Sand the sawn edges of the notches smooth.

Cut rabbets in the sides for the back

To complete the sides, cut a rabbet in each back edge to accept the $1/4$" plywood back. This rabbet is $3/8$" wide and $1/4$" deep. Install a dado set in the table saw and bury the blade in an auxiliary fence as shown in the bottom photo. Cut the rabbet the full length on each side. When done, cut the shelves to width and length. Note that they're $1/2$" narrower than the sides. This allows for the back and the shelf supports added later.

Assemble the case

Now you can assemble the case. Apply a generous bead of glue inside the rabbet and dadoes on one side. Insert the shelves so the back edges are aligned with the front edge of the lengthwise rabbet for the $\frac{1}{4}$" plywood back. Apply glue in the rabbet and dadoes in the remaining side, and fit this over the shelves. Stand the bookcase up, and apply clamps across the shelves as shown in the top photo. Measure diagonally from one corner to the opposite corner. Do the same for the other diagonal, and compare measurements. If they're the same, the case if square. If not, the case is racked and you'll need to adjust clamp position or clamp pressure to bring the case into square.

Install the back

Allow the clamped case to dry overnight and then cut the $\frac{1}{4}$" plywood back to size. Remove the clamps from the case and place it face down on your work surface. Apply a bead of glue in the lengthwise rabbets in the sides and along the back edges of the shelves. Set the back in place and attach it to the sides and shelves with 1" brads (middle photo). Let the glue set up at least 1 hour before proceeding.

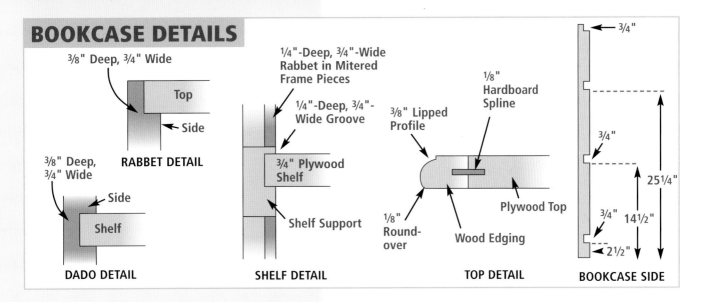

BOOKCASE DETAILS

RABBET DETAIL
- 3/8" Deep, 3/4" Wide
- Top
- Side

DADO DETAIL
- 3/8" Deep, 3/4" Wide
- Side
- Shelf

SHELF DETAIL
- 1/4"-Deep, 3/4"-Wide Rabbet in Mitered Frame Pieces
- 1/4"-Deep, 3/4"-Wide Groove
- 3/4" Plywood Shelf
- Shelf Support

TOP DETAIL
- 3/8" Lipped Profile
- 1/8" Hardboard Spline
- 1/8" Round-over
- Wood Edging
- Plywood Top

BOOKCASE SIDE
- 3/4"
- 3/4"
- 25 1/4"
- 3/4" 14 1/2"
- 2 1/2"

Make the face frame pieces

The face frame pieces that cover the exposed plywood edges are cut from $3/4$" stock to a width of $1^1/2$". Measure the front of the cabinet and miter-cut four pieces to fit, as shown in the top photo. To make it easier to clamp these in place, next cut a $1/4$" × $3/4$-wide rabbet on the inside face of each mitered piece along the outside edge. This way the mitered pieces will lock into place when installed. Cut the shelf supports to width now (they're also $1^1/2$" wide), and leave them a bit long so you can trim them to fit once the mitered frame pieces are installed. A groove is cut on the inside face of each support to fit over the front edge of each shelf (see the shelf detail drawing on page 167).

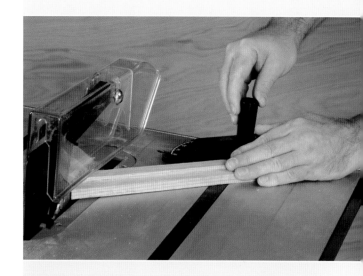

Attach the face frame to the case

Although we simply glued the face frame pieces to the front edges of the case, you can also use nails. Work on one mitered piece at a time and apply glue to the mating edge of the case. Position the mitered frame piece on the case so the edge is flush with the side face. Apply clamps until the glue dries, as shown in the middle photo. Repeat for the remaining mitered frame pieces. Then measure from frame side to frame side, and trim the shelf supports to fit. Apply glue to the edge of the shelf and press the support onto the shelf. Set a heavy weight (such as a toolbox) onto the support until the glue dries; repeat for the remaining shelf support. You can also attach the toe kick at this time with glue and 2" finish nails.

Cut a spline groove in the top

All that's left is to make and install the top. The top is made of $3/4$" plywood, and the edges are concealed with wood edging held in place with splines. Cut the top to size and then cut grooves ($1/8$" kerfs) in the front and side edges. Attach a tall auxiliary fence to your rip fence to support the top, and position the rip fence to center the kerf in the edge of the plywood. Adjust the blade height for a $3/8$"-deep cut, and cut the kerfs as shown in the bottom photo.

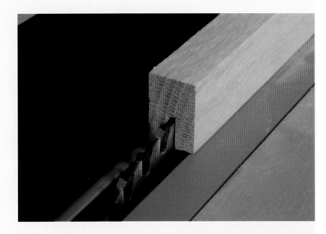

Cut spline grooves in the edging

Cut the edging that wraps around the front and side edges of the top to a width of $1^1/8$" and to rough length. Use the setup as you did to kerf the top to cut grooves in the edging pieces, as shown in the top photo. This way the kerfs will line up perfectly.

Add the edging

Cut $1/8$" hardboard splines to a width of $3/4$" and to rough length. Before you apply glue, do a test run to make sure everything fits. When it does, apply a bead of glue inside the grooves (kerfs) and to the edges of the plywood top and edging. Assemble the edging onto the top, and apply clamps as shown in the middle photo. After the glue has dried, remove the clamps and scrape or sand off any dried glue. Then rout a decorative edge on the edging, as shown in the inset photo. Rout a $3/8$" lipped round-over on the top edge and a $1/8$" round-over on the bottom edge, as illustrated in the top detail drawing on page 167.

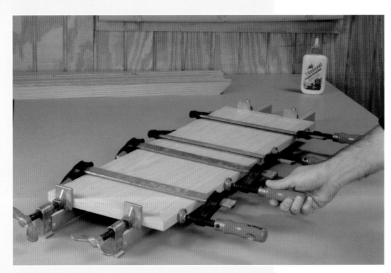

Attach top to the case

To complete the bookcase, position the top so that it's centered from side to side on the case and flush with the back edge. Secure the top to the case by driving #8 × $1^1/4$" woodscrews up through the top shelf and into the top, as shown in the bottom photo; you may find that a stubby screwdriver is needed to do this. Then sand the entire project and apply the finish of your choice.

Blanket Chest

Whether it's used to store blankets, clothes, or toys, the blanket chest shown here will instantly add storage space to any room. Its large interior measures 13" × 20" × 36". That's almost 5½ cubic feet of storage. The shapely legs are actually two pieces that are mitered and joined together with splines. The plywood sides and front and back are joined to the leg with stub-tenon-and-groove joinery. Stub-tenon-and-groove joinery is easy to cut and holds up well over time (for more on this joint, see pages 84–85).

The lid of the chest is made of plywood, and the front and back plywood edges are covered with thin edging strips. The ends are also covered with edging that's often called breadboard ends. The lid is heavy and so is attached to the case with a single long piano hinge. It's supported on the inside with a lid support that will hold it in the open position if desired.

EXPLODED VIEW

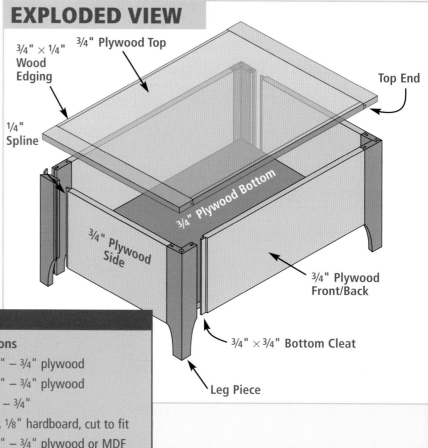

3/4" × 1/4" Wood Edging

3/4" Plywood Top

Top End

1/4" Spline

3/4" Plywood Bottom

3/4" Plywood Side

3/4" Plywood Front/Back

3/4" × 3/4" Bottom Cleat

Leg Piece

MATERIALS LIST

Part	Quantity	Dimensions
Front/back	2	14" × 32" – 3/4" plywood
Sides	2	14" × 16" – 3/4" plywood
Leg pieces	8	3" × 20" – 3/4"
Splines	4	1/2"-wide, 1/8" hardboard, cut to fit
Bottom	1	20" × 36" – 3/4" plywood or MDF
Bottom cleats	4	3/4" × 3/4" – cut to fit
Top	1	21½" × 36" – 3/4" plywood
Top edging	2	3/4" × 21½" – 1/4"
Top ends	2	2" × 22" – 3/4"
Hinge	1	1½" piano hinge, 36" long
Lid support	1	brass with adjustable stop

Bevel-rip the leg pieces

To begin work on the blanket chest, start by cutting the leg pieces to size, see the exploded view and materials list on page 170. To give the legs the look of a solid piece, the leg parts are joined with long miters. Angle your saw blade to 45 degrees and position the rip fence to bevel the edge; make sure to position the rip fence so the blade tilts away from it. Raise the blade to cut through the stock, and turn on the saw. Use a push stick to slide each leg piece past the blade, as shown in the top photo.

Cut grooves for the splines

Although you could simply glue the leg pieces together now, you'd find it difficult to keep the pieces aligned and end up with a tight miter. Also, a long miter like this fails to offer any mechanical strength. Both of these problems can be solved by joining the parts with splines. To cut the grooves (or kerfs) for the splines, tilt your blade to 45 degrees and position the rip fence to cut the kerf $1/2$" in from the miter point, as shown in the middle photo and illustrated in the spline detail drawing on page 172. Cut grooves on each of the mitered edges of all eight leg pieces.

Cut joinery grooves in the leg pieces

Before you can glue up the legs, there are a few more things to do. First, cut $1/4$"-wide grooves in the unmitered edges to accept the stub tenons that will be cut later in the chest sides, front, and back. And second, shape the legs as illustrated on page 172. Install a $1/4$"-wide dado set in the saw and raise the blade to cut $3/8$" deep. Position the rip fence to make a centered groove and cut a groove in each of the eight leg pieces, as shown in the bottom photo. Alternatively, you can cut centered grooves using a standard blade and the technique described on page 73.

Shape the legs

To create a gentle foot for each leg, a curved portion is removed at the bottom of each leg piece. As there are eight leg pieces, consider making a leg pattern out of a piece of $^1/8$" hardboard or plastic laminate (see the leg pattern drawing below). Lay out the curve on each piece, taking care to align the pattern with the grooved edge of the leg piece so it's flush with the bottom. Trace the shape on the leg; make sure you make four book-matched sets. Then cut the shape with a saber saw or band saw as shown in the top photo. Sand the curve smooth with a dowel wrapped in sandpaper, or with a sanding drum fitted in the drill press.

Glue up the legs

Now you can glue up book-matched pairs of leg pieces to form the four legs. Working on one leg at a time, apply glue to the grooves (kerfs) for the spline. Apply glue to the mitered edges of each leg piece. Insert a spline in one leg piece and slip the other piece over the spline. To help align everything and make it easy to clamp, butt a scrap of 4×4 (or two 2×4s screwed together) against the inside faces of the leg, as shown in the middle photo. This way you apply clamps to pull the miter tight. Once the leg is dry, repeat this procedure for the other three legs.

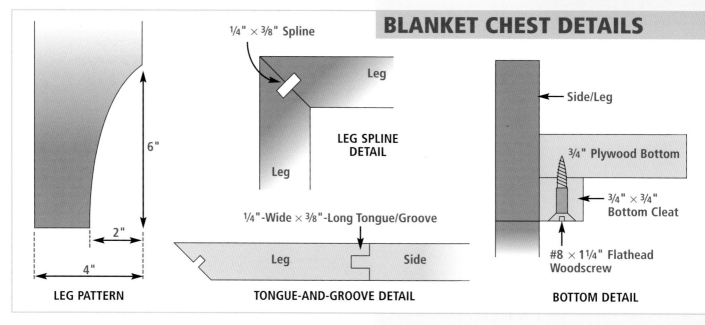

BLANKET CHEST DETAILS

LEG PATTERN

6"
2"
4"

LEG SPLINE DETAIL

$^1/4$" × $^3/8$" Spline
Leg
Leg

$^1/4$"-Wide × $^3/8$"-Long Tongue/Groove

TONGUE-AND-GROOVE DETAIL

Leg
Side

BOTTOM DETAIL

Side/Leg
$^3/4$" Plywood Bottom
$^3/4$" × $^3/4$" Bottom Cleat
#8 × 1$^1/4$" Flathead Woodscrew

Cut stub tenons on the chest parts

With the legs complete, you can work on the chest sides, front, and back. Cut these parts to size per the materials list on page 170. Then cut stub tenons on the ends of each piece. Install a dado set in the saw and bury the blade in an auxiliary fence. Adjust blade height to make a $1/4$"-thick tenon. Position the rip fence to create a $3/8$"-long tenon. Turn on the saw and push the end of each piece past the dado set. Flip the piece over and cut the other face to form the tenon as shown in the top photo. Repeat for the other end and the remaining pieces.

Assemble the chest

After the stub tenons are cut, you can assemble the chest. Start by gluing a pair of legs onto a chest side so the side is flush with the tops of the legs. Then glue up the opposite end. When this is dry, apply glue to the grooves in the legs and slip the front and back in place, making sure that the top edges are flush with the tops of the legs. The best way to do this is to assemble the chest upside down on a flat work surface, as shown in the middle photo. Apply bar clamps from one end to the other and measure diagonals. If they're not the same, the chest is not square and you'll need to adjust either the position or the pressure on one or more clamps to rack the chest back into square.

Add the cleats for the bottom

When the glue has dried completely, remove the clamps and cut the bottom cleat stock to size. This is just $3/4$" × $3/4$" stock cut to fit inside the chest along the bottom edges of the sides and front and back. Attach the cleats to the chest with glue and clamps so that they end up flush with the bottom edges of the sides, front, and back, as shown in the bottom photo, and illustrated in the bottom detail drawing on page 172.

Add the bottom

Now you can add the bottom to the chest. Measure the inside width and length, and cut a piece of $3/4$" plywood or MDF to fit. Slip the bottom in place as shown in the top photo, and then secure it to the bottom cleats with #$8 \times 1^1/4$" woodscrews. Drill pilot holes through the bottom and into the cleats, as illustrated in the bottom detail drawing on page 172.

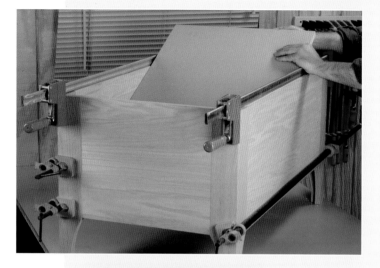

Cut joinery grooves in the top ends

All that's left is to make and install the top. Start by cutting the top, top edging, and top ends to size, per the materials list on page 170. The top ends attach to the top with stub-tenon-and-groove joinery. Cut the grooves along the long inside edge of each of the top ends with a $1/4$" dado set, installed in the table saw set to a height of $3/8$", as shown in the middle photo at right.

Make the top

Before you can cut the stub tenons on the ends of the top, you'll need to cover the exposed plywood edges on the front and back. To do this, glue the $1/4$"-thick top edging to the top, as shown in the bottom photo. Make sure that the edging is flush with the good face. Once the glue has dried, remove the clamps and sand the edging flush with the top on both faces. Then cut stub tenons on the ends of the top. Bury a dado set in the rip fence and adjust it to fit the grooves that you cut earlier in the top ends, as shown in the inset photo above.

Glue the top ends to the top

Once stub tenons have been cut on the top, attach the ends. Apply glue inside the grooves the full length of the top ends. Note: Since plywood is so dimensionally stable, you can glue the tongue into the full length of the groove. If you were to use solid wood for the top, you'd need to fasten the end to the top only at the middle so the top could expand and contract as the humidity changed. Clamp the top ends in place as shown in the top photo. Once the glue has dried, remove the clamps and sand the entire chest inside and out.

Install the lid hinge

The lid attaches to the chest with a 36"-long piano hinge. Start by centering this hinge from side to side on the back top edge of the chest. Drill pilot holes at the ends and install the screws. Next drill the remaining holes and install all the screws for the bottom hinge flap, as shown in the middle photo. Then flip the chest on its back and butt the lid up against the back so the top hinge flap is centered on the lid from side to side. Drill pilot holes and secure the hinge to the lid with the screws provided.

Add the lid support

Finally, install the support if desired to hold the lid in the open position. Start by attaching it to the inside face of one of the sides with the screws provided. Then hold the lid open at 90 degrees and pull the support up until it contacts the lid. Mark the hole locations, drill pilot holes, and secure the top of the support to the lid with the screws provided, as shown in the bottom photo. Test for smooth operation and adjust the tension so the lid doesn't slam shut if dropped. Note: If you don't want the plywood edges of the sides, front, and back exposed, consider applying edging to the top edges only, as you did with the lid before cutting the stub tenons. If you do this, you'll need to reduce the width of the sides, front, and back by $1/4$", to $13 3/4$".

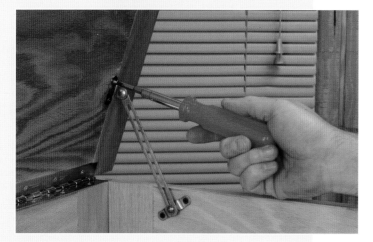

Wall-Hung Tool Cabinet

This all-purpose wall-hung storage cabinet will work equally well holding tools and supplies in the shop, sports gear in the garage, or cleaning supplies in the laundry room. The cabinet is made of $^3/4$" plywood joined together with a locking rabbet. The door frame parts are joined similarly. The cabinet is divided in two by a vertical center partition, and adjustable shelves are supported by shelf pins inserted in a set of holes drilled in the sides and middle divider. The back of the cabinet and the panels for the doors are $^1/2$"-thick plywood so that you can mount tool hangers or hang other items directly on them.

The doors open and close on a set of full-length piano hinges, so there's never any worry about sagging. One of the niftiest features of this cabinet is hidden from view. A unique, beveled cleat and hanger system makes it easy to hang the cabinet on any wall; see the hanger/cleat detail drawing on page 178 to see how this works. We used $^1/2$" and $^3/4$" birch plywood for the cabinet and $^3/4$" birch for the solid-wood parts.

EXPLODED VIEW

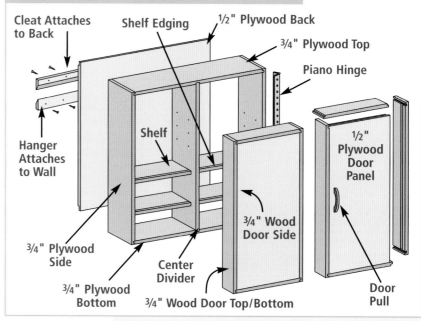

Cleat Attaches to Back · Shelf Edging · $^1/2$" Plywood Back · $^3/4$" Plywood Top · Piano Hinge · Hanger Attaches to Wall · Shelf · $^1/2$" Plywood Door Panel · $^3/4$" Wood Door Side · $^3/4$" Plywood Side · Center Divider · $^3/4$" Plywood Bottom · $^3/4$" Wood Door Top/Bottom · Door Pull

MATERIALS LIST

Part	Quantity	Dimensions	Part	Quantity	Dimensions
Case top/bottom	2	8" × 36" − $^3/4$" plywood	Case hanger	1	1$^3/4$" × 40" − $^3/4$"
Case sides	2	8" × 42" − $^3/4$" plywood	Door tops/bottoms	4	2$^1/2$" × 17$^7/16$" − $^3/4$"
Center divider	1	7$^1/4$" × 41$^1/2$" − $^3/4$" plywood	Door sides	4	2$^1/2$" × 42" − $^3/4$"
Shelves	6	7" × 17$^1/4$" − $^3/4$" plywood	Door panels	2	17$^1/4$" × 41$^1/4$" − $^1/2$" plywood
Shelf edging	6	$^3/4$" × 17$^1/4$" − $^1/4$"	Door hinges	2	1$^1/2$" × 42" piano hinge
Case back	1	35$^1/2$" × 41" − $^1/2$" plywood	Door pulls	2	3"
Case cleat	1	1$^3/4$" × 40" − $^3/4$"	Shelf pins	24	$^1/4$" posts

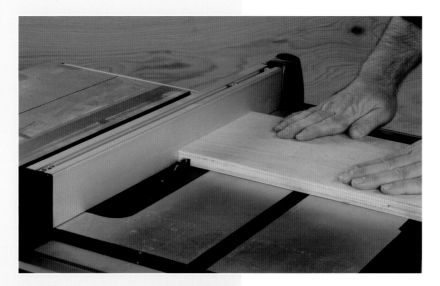

Cut grooves in the sides for the locking rabbets

To build the wall-hung tool cabinet, begin by cutting the cabinet sides, top, and bottom to size (see the exploded view and materials list on page 176). The sides are joined to the top and bottom with a $3/8" \times 3/8"$ locking rabbet, see the joinery detail drawing on page 178. Start by cutting the grooves on the inside faces at the ends of each side piece, as shown in the top photo. A $3/8"$-wide dado set in the table saw will make quick work of these.

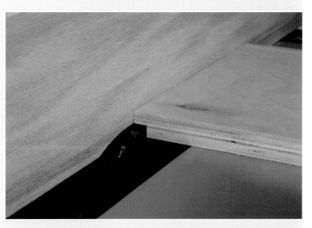

Cut the rabbets in the top and bottom

Now you can cut rabbets in the ends of the top and bottom that will form the tongues that fit into the grooves you just cut in the sides. Install a $1/2"$-wide dado set in your saw and bury it in an auxiliary fence. Adjust the blade height and rip fence to create a tongue that fits snug in the grooves in the sides, as shown in the middle photo. Flip the piece end for end and cut the other end; repeat for the other top/bottom piece.

Cut the dadoes for the center divider

The center divider fits into dadoes cut on the inside face of the top and bottom. Install a $3/4"$-wide dado set and adjust the blade for a $3/8"$-deep cut. Position the rip fence to center the dado and then cut the dado in the top and in the bottom, taking care to reference the same end so that the dadoes align, as shown in the bottom photo.

Make the back

Since the cabinet is hung from the back, the back needs to be securely fastened to the cabinet. To do this, we used a variation of the locking rabbet joint similar to the one shown below to join the door panel to the door side. Start by cutting a 1/4"-wide groove, 1/4" in from the back edge of the cabinet top, bottom, and sides, as shown in the top photo. When you've cut this in all four pieces, cut the back to size and rabbet the edge to form a tongue to fit into the grooves you just cut.

Add the back

At this point, you can start assembling the cabinet. Because of all the locking rabbets, the cabinet must be assembled in a set sequence. Start by gluing one side to the bottom. Apply glue to the groove in the side and slip the parts together. Then apply glue to the groove in the side and the bottom for the back. Slide the back into place, taking care to orient the tongue correctly, as shown in the middle photo.

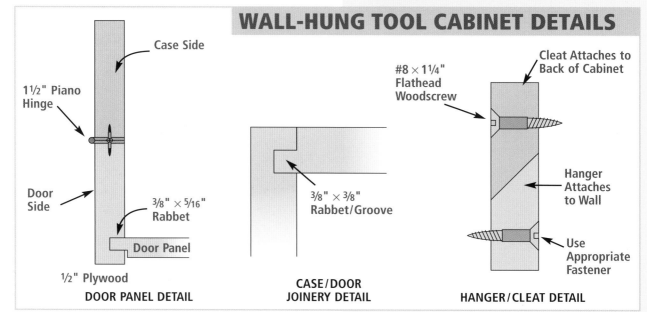

WALL-HUNG TOOL CABINET DETAILS

Case Side

1¹/₂" Piano Hinge

Door Side

³/₈" × ⁵/₁₆" Rabbet

Door Panel

¹/₂" Plywood

DOOR PANEL DETAIL

³/₈" × ³/₈" Rabbet/Groove

CASE/DOOR JOINERY DETAIL

#8 × 1¹/₄" Flathead Woodscrew

Cleat Attaches to Back of Cabinet

Hanger Attaches to Wall

Use Appropriate Fastener

HANGER/CLEAT DETAIL

Add the remaining side and the top

With the back in place, you can add the remaining side and the top. Apply glue to the grooves in both parts. Then slip the side in place and set the top on the back so the tongue on the back fits into the groove in the back. Hold the side with one hand and pull it out far enough so the tongue on the end of the top slips into the groove on the end of the side. Once together, apply clamps across the cabinet, as shown in the top photo. Measure the diagonals and adjust clamp position or pressure as needed to make them match, assuring that the cabinet is square.

Install the center divider

Let the cabinet sit overnight and then remove the clamps. Measure between the bottoms of the centered dadoes on the top and bottom, and cut a divider to length. Apply glue in the dadoes and slide the center divider in place, as shown in the middle photo. Once it bottoms out, you can drive a few nails into the divider from the top and bottom to help hold it in place. Alternatively, you can apply clamps and allow the glue to dry.

Cut the grooves in the door sides

The cabinet is basically finished now, so you can begin work on the doors. The sides and top and bottom of the doors are joined with locking rabbets just like the cabinet sides, top, and bottom; see the cabinet/door joinery detail shown on page 178. Make the grooves in the sides by installing a 3/8"-wide dado set in the saw and adjust the height for a 3/8"-deep cut. Position the rip fence as a stop and guide the door side past the blade, using the miter gauge and a backer block to prevent tear-out, as shown in the bottom photo.

Cut rabbets on the door tops and bottoms

Now you can cut the rabbets on the door tops and bottoms to form a tongue to fit in the grooves you just cut in the door sides. Install a $1/2$"-dado set in the table saw and adjust it for a $3/8$"-deep cut. Bury the blade in an auxiliary fence and position it for a $3/8$"-wide cut. Then cut the rabbets on the door parts as shown in the top photo. Test the fit in the grooves in the sides — it should be snug; if it's not, adjust as needed.

Form the tongues on the door panels

The next step is to install a $1/4$" dado set in the saw and cut a groove along the length of each of the door frame parts on the inside face, as shown in the middle photo and the detail drawing on page 178. This groove will accept the rabbeted door panels. Cut the door panels to size and rabbet the edges to form tongues that will fit in the grooves you just cut in the door sides, top, and bottom.

Assemble the doors

To assemble the doors, work on one at a time. Begin by applying glue to the locking rabbet grooves and the grooves for the door panels. Attach one door side to the door bottom and slip the door panel in place. Then add the remaining door side and the top. Apply clamps and measure the diagonals as shown in the bottom photo. If the diagonals don't match, rack the door by adjusting the clamp position or pressure until it's square. Repeat for the second door.

Attach the doors to the cabinet

After the glue on both doors has dried, remove the clamps and attach them to the cabinet. They're attached with 42"-long lengths of piano hinge. These come in a standard length of 48", so you'll have to measure and cut them to length with a hacksaw; file the ends smooth. To attach the doors, begin by securing one hinge flap to the door. Clamp it in place temporarily and drill pilot holes for screws at the ends and middle. Install these screws, drill pilot holes for the remaining screws, and drive them in. Then set the cabinet upright on your work surface and position the door next to it so that it butts up against the side, as shown in the top photo. Clamp the door to the side, drill pilot holes, and install the screws. Repeat for the other door.

Glue on the shelf edging

Cut the shelves to size and then cover the front exposed plywood edge with strips of the shelf edging. The edging is just $1/4$"-thick, $3/4$"-wide strips of matching wood (see pages 50–51 for tips on cutting narrow stock such as this). The edging strips are simply glued in place. Apply a generous bead of glue to the front edge of a shelf and clamp the edging so it's flush with the face of the shelf, as shown in the middle photo. Allow to dry and repeat for the remaining shelves. When all are dry, scrape off any excess glue and sand the edging smooth with the face of each shelf.

Bevel-rip the hanger and cleat

The cabinet is mounted to the wall with a simple beveled-cleat-and-hanger system, see the detail drawing on page 178. To make both of these, start by cutting a strip of wood $3^1/8$" wide and 40" long. Then tilt your saw blade to 45 degrees and position the rip fence to cut this blank perfectly in half. Turn on the saw and, using a push stick, push the blank past the blade as shown in the bottom photo.

Attach the cleat to the cabinet back

To use this hanging system, begin by attaching the cleat to the back of the cabinet, as shown in the top photo. In order to work, the point of the bevel must be facing down and away from the cabinet as shown. Apply glue along the length of the cleat and then clamp it to the top edge of the back. Go around to the front of the cabinet, open the doors, and drive #8 × 1" woodscrews through the back and into the cleat. Space the screws about 6" apart, starting roughly 2" in from each end of the cleat. Allow the glue to dry.

Mount the hanger on the wall

While the glue attaching the cleat to the cabinet is drying, you can position and mount the hanger to your wall. Start by locating the wall studs with an electronic stud finder; mark their positions on the wall. Then position the hanger on the wall at the desired height and use a level to level the hanger on the wall, as shown in the middle photo. The point of the hanger must be pointing up and away from the wall as shown. Secure the hanger to the wall by driving 3" screws through the hanger and into the studs. If necessary, use Molly or toggle bolts for added support.

Add the door pulls

After adding the hanger system, the next step is to add the pulls to the doors. Lay them out centered on the door from top to bottom and $2\frac{1}{2}$" in from the inside edge of each door. Use the pulls to locate and mark the mounting screw locations, and drill pilot holes through the door panels. Attach the pulls with the screws provided, as shown in the bottom photo.

Drill holes for the shelf pins

The final task to complete the cabinet is to install the shelves. The shelves are held in place with metal shelf support pins. These typically use $1/4$"-round posts that fit into $1/4$"-diameter holes. To space the holes so they'll all align, use a scrap of $1/4$" pegboard as a drilling template. Cut a scrap piece to size and clamp it to the inside face of the cabinet. Mark sets of holes for the shelf supports, and then fit a $1/4$" drill bit with a stop to prevent the bit from drilling through the plywood. Set the stop for a $5/16$"-deep hole, and drill at each of the marked locations on the pegboard, as shown in the top photo. Drill sets of holes approximately every 3" from top to bottom for maximum flexibility. Also keep the holes as far apart as possible while still staying about 1" in from the front and back of the sides; this will support the shelf the best. When you've drilled one set of holes, slide the pegboard over to the center divider, keeping the back edge against the back. Clamp it in place and drill through the same set of holes. Repeat for the other side.

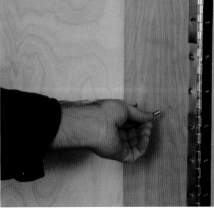

Add the shelf pins

After you've drilled all the holes for the shelf pins, vacuum out the cabinet and install the pins by pushing them into the holes, as shown in the middle photo.

Install the shelves

Finally, place the shelves in the cabinet at the desired locations, as shown in the bottom photo. Note that on some shelf pins, the flat part that the shelf rests on often has a hole drilled in it. This hole lets you secure the shelf to the pin by driving a $1/2$" screw up through the bottom of the shelf pin and into the shelf.

Occasional Table

The design of this easy-to-make occasional table is based on a taboret table manufactured by Gustav Stickley in the early 1900s. It features a round top, exposed through tenons, and cross-lapped rails. Although Stickley would have made this out of quartersawn white oak, almost any hardwood will do (we used plain-sawn red oak here). The clean lines of this table will make it suitable for a wide variety of decors.

What makes this project particularly easy to build is that there are no mortises or tenons to cut — even though the table is assembled with mortise-and-tenon joints throughout. Instead, by gluing up the legs from separate pieces, you can leave spaces that will become the mortises. The ends of the brackets fit through these "faux" mortises without need of tenons. The brackets are pegged in place in the mortises with wood dowels; the resulting table is quite stout.

EXPLODED VIEW

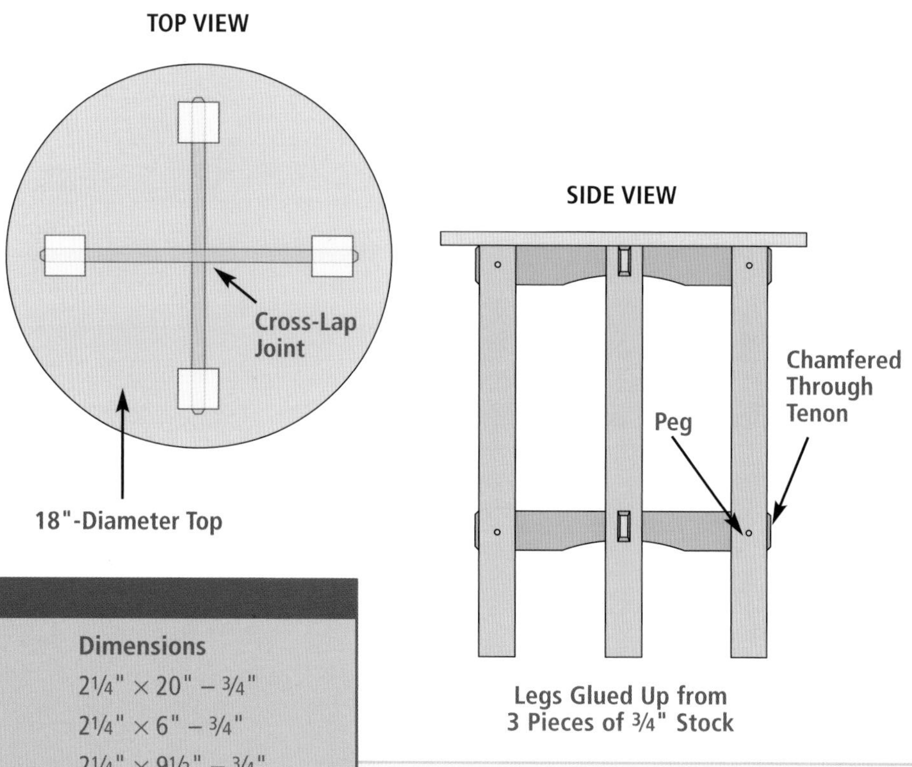

TOP VIEW

Cross-Lap Joint

18"-Diameter Top

SIDE VIEW

Peg

Chamfered Through Tenon

Legs Glued Up from 3 Pieces of ³⁄₄" Stock

MATERIALS LIST

Part	Quantity	Dimensions
Outer leg sections	8	2¼" × 20" − ¾"
Inner leg bottoms	4	2¼" × 6" − ¾"
Inner leg tops	4	2¼" × 9½" − ¾"
Top brackets	2	2¼" × 14½" − ¾"
Bottom brackets	2	2¼" × 14½" − ¾"
Top	1	18" diameter − ¾"
Pins	18	¼" dowel

Cut the leg parts to length

Each leg is made up of four parts: two identical outer leg sections, an inner leg top, and an inner leg bottom (see the exploded view and materials list on page 184). Cut the leg pieces to a width of $2^{1}/4"$ and to the lengths specified in the materials list, as shown in the top photo. Note: You may want to cut these pieces a bit wider (say, $2^{1}/2"$) so that you can clean up the edges with a hand plane, jointer, or power planer after they've been glued up.

Glue up the legs

Once all the leg pieces are cut to size, you can glue the legs up one at a time. Apply glue generously to both faces of the inner leg top and bottom. Sandwich these between the outer leg sections, taking care to leave the appropriate spaces for mortises; see the leg detail drawing on page 186. See below for a guaranteed way to create perfect mortises. Apply clamps as shown in the middle photo, and allow each leg section to dry overnight.

Guaranteed mortise spacing

To create perfect mortises for the bracket ends, use scraps of $2^{1}/4"$-wide stock as "keys" to space apart the inner leg top and bottom, as shown in the bottom photo. To keep glue from sticking to the keys, apply a coat of varnish. to the keys When dry, rub a little paste wax on the face and edges of each key. Also, as soon as you have a leg clamped together, drive the key out with a mallet so it doesn't accidentally get glued in place.

Repeat this for the three remaining legs. After the legs are dry, remove any glue/irregularities by passing the legs over a jointer or planer or by hand-planing them smooth. Continue until each leg is exactly $2^{1}/4"$ square. Then rout a $^{1}/8"$-chamfer on all four edges of each leg and on the bottom of each leg (don't chamfer the tops).

Cut the notches on the brackets

The brackets are the most complicated part of this project, but they're still pretty simple. The secret is to cut the cross-lap notches before you shape the curve on the bottom edges. Cut four bracket pieces to $2^1/4" \times 14^1/2"$ from $^3/4"$ stock. Then lay out and cut the notches for the cross laps. These must be centered exactly for this to work. The best way to do this is on the table saw with a dado blade, using the rip fence as a stop, as shown in the top photo. Both notches are $^3/4"$ wide, and the notch on the top bracket is $1^1/2"$ deep, while the notch on the bottom bracket is $^3/4"$ deep (see the detail drawing below). Make test cuts on scraps before committing to your finished pieces.

Cut the curves on the brackets

Next, you can lay out the gentle curve on the bottom of each bracket. The curve starts $4^3/4"$ in from each end and is $^3/4"$ high in the center. It's best to make a template for this so they'll all be similar. Cut these curves with a saber saw or band saw as shown in the middle photo. If you're using a band saw, you can double these up easily to cut the curves. Sand the curves smooth with a dowel wrapped in sandpaper, or with a sanding drum fitted in the drill press.

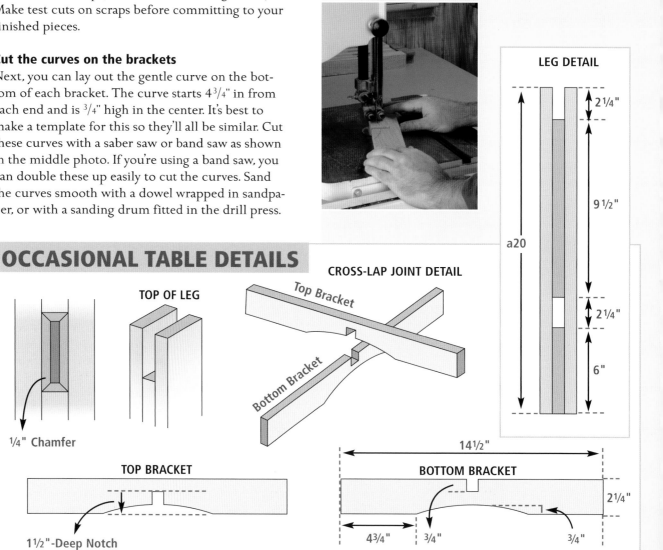

OCCASIONAL TABLE DETAILS

TOP OF LEG

$^1/4"$ Chamfer

CROSS-LAP JOINT DETAIL

Top Bracket

Bottom Bracket

LEG DETAIL

$2^1/4"$

$9^1/2"$

a20

$2^1/4"$

6"

TOP BRACKET

$1^1/2"$-Deep Notch

BOTTOM BRACKET

$14^1/2"$

$4^3/4"$ $^3/4"$ $^3/4"$

$2^1/4"$

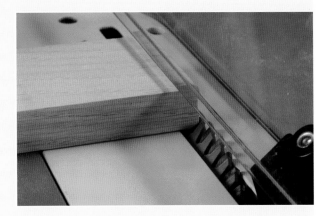

Chamfer the ends of brackets

Once the bracket curves are cut, there are a few more things to do before they can be assembled. First, cut a ¼" chamfer on the ends of each bracket, as shown in the top photo and illustrated in the detail drawing on page 186. Next, drill counterbored shank holes 4" in from each end, on the underside of the top set of brackets that will sit in the mortises on top of the legs. These holes will be used later to secure the top. Make them slightly oversized so that the screws can move along with the top as it expands and contracts with changes in humidity.

Glue the bracket sections together

Now you can assemble pairs of brackets to make the top and bottom bracket assemblies. Apply a generous bead of glue to the inside faces of both notches cut in a pair of brackets. Then fit the pieces together and apply a clamp to hold them in place, as shown in the middle photo. Check the intersecting brackets with a try square to make sure all is square, and adjust if necessary. Allow each bracket assembly to dry overnight before proceeding.

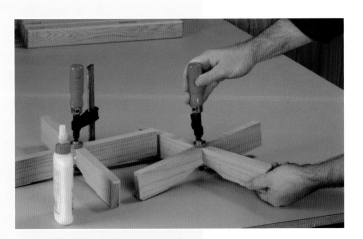

Pin the brackets

After the glue has completely dried in each bracket assembly, drill ¼"-diameter holes for pins in the underside of each bracket assembly where the brackets intersect. Then apply a dollop of glue in the hole and drive in a length of ¼" dowel, as shown in the bottom photo. These dowel pins help reinforce the joint and will keep them locked together over time.

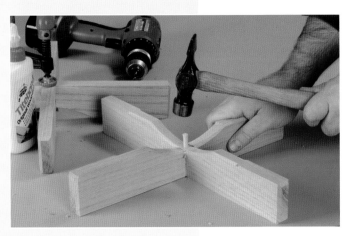

Glue the legs to the bottom brackets

With the bracket assemblies pinned, you can start assembling the table. Begin by applying glue to the inside edges of the bottom mortises in a pair of legs. Then slide the legs over the ends of the brackets. As the brackets slide though the mortises, they'll distribute the glue along the insides of the mortise. Repeat this for the remaining pair of legs. Check to make sure each leg is plumb and that the brackets protrude so only the chamfered ends are exposed. Apply clamps to the legs as shown in the top photo to help hold everything in place until the glue dries.

Glue the legs to the top brackets

After the glue has dried, add the top bracket assembly to the legs. This unit is easier to glue and install, as the mortises are "open." Apply glue with a brush to the inside faces of the mortises, and set the top bracket in place. Again, make sure the brackets are protruding only far enough to leave the chamfered ends of the brackets exposed. When everything looks good, apply clamps as shown in the middle photo and let the glue dry overnight.

Pin the legs to the brackets

As added insurance against movement, drill pilot holes and install pins in each mortise location. Drill ¼"-diameter holes centered on the width of the legs and centered from top to bottom on each mortise. You can drill stopped holes as we did here, or drill completely through each leg. Once you've drilled a hole, dribble a little glue in the hole and drive in a ¼" dowel, as shown in the bottom photo. Cut off any excess with a fine-tooth saw, and then use a chisel to pare the end of the dowel flush with the leg face. Repeat for the remaining seven mortises.

Make the top

The top is glued up from several pieces of ³/₄" stock. Cut sufficient stock to create a blank that's at least 20" square. If desired, use biscuits or dowels to align the pieces; just make sure to keep the biscuits or dowels away from the perimeter of the top. Clamp up the top and allow it to dry overnight.

Then clean off any excess glue and mark the center of the top, using diagonals. Use a trammel point or a large compass to lay out an 18" circle. Cut the top to shape with a saber saw, or use a band saw as shown in the upper photo. Sand the edges and top smooth. Then rout a ¹/₄" chamfer around the top edge only.

Attach the top to the top brackets

All that's left is to attach the top to the top brackets. The screws used here will pass through the holes you drilled earlier in the ends of the top bracket assembly. Make sure to select screws that are long enough to secure the top in place but that will not poke through the top when fully driven in.

Center the top from front to back and from side to side on the base. Drive a screw in at one end of a bracket, as shown in the lower photo, and then drive one in on the opposite end of the bracket. Repeat for the remaining bracket. Finally, sand the entire project and apply the finish of your choice.

INDEX

METRIC EQUIVALENCY CHART

Inches to millimeters and centimeters

inches	mm	cm	inches	cm	inches	cm
1/8	3	0.3	9	22.9	30	76.2
1/4	6	0.6	10	25.4	31	78.7
3/8	10	1.0	11	27.9	32	81.3
1/2	13	1.3	12	30.5	33	83.8
5/8	16	1.6	13	33.0	34	86.4
3/4	19	1.9	14	35.6	35	88.9
7/8	22	2.2	15	38.1	36	91.4
1	25	2.5	16	40.6	37	94.0
1 1/4	32	3.2	17	43.2	38	96.5
1 1/2	38	3.8	18	45.7	39	99.1
1 3/4	44	4.4	19	48.3	40	101.6
2	51	5.1	20	50.8	41	104.1
2 1/2	64	6.4	21	53.3	42	106.7
3	76	7.6	22	55.9	43	109.2
3 1/2	89	8.9	23	58.4	44	111.8
4	102	10.2	24	61.0	45	114.3
4 1/2	114	11.4	25	63.5	46	116.8
5	127	12.7	26	66.0	47	119.4
6	152	15.2	27	68.6	48	121.9
7	178	17.8	28	71.1	49	124.5
8	203	20.3	29	73.7	50	127.0

mm = millimeters   cm = centimeters

Table Saw photo credits

Photo courtesy of August Home Publishing Co. (www.woodsmithstore.com): page 34 (bottom).

Photo courtesy of Biesemeyer (biesemeyer.com): page 31 (top).

Photos courtesy of Bench Dog, Inc. (www.benchdog.com): page 30 (middle), page 33 (bottom).

Photos courtesy of Delta Woodworking Tools (deltawoodworking.com): page 10 (top), page 30 (top inset), page 32 (top), page 32 (middle right), page 34 (top).

Photo courtesy of DeWalt Tools (www.dewalt.com): page 9 (top).

Photos courtesy of Freud, Inc. (www.freudtools.com): page 26 (all), page 27 (bottom), page 28 (top).

Photo courtesy of Incra (www.incra.com): page 34 (middle).

Photos courtesy of Jet Equipment and Tools (www.jettools.com): page 30 (top right and bottom), page 31 (bottom), page 57 (top).

Photo courtesy of Powermatic Tools (www.jettools.com): page 11 (top).

Photos courtesy of SawStop (www.sawstop.com): page 18 (both bottom).

Photo courtesy of Skil-Bosch Corporation (www.boschtools.com): page 17 Bottom left).

Photo courtesy of Triton (www.triton.net.au): page 35 (bottom).